The Black Experience in
Revolutionary North Carolina

For Robert F. Durden—
gentleman, scholar, teacher, friend

The Black Experience in Revolutionary North Carolina

Jeffrey J. Crow

Raleigh

Division of Archives and History
North Carolina Department of Cultural Resources

Fourth Printing, 1996

CONTENTS

PREFACE

Writing a study of the black experience in Revolutionary North Carolina raises many questions for the historian and more than a few problems. Because the institution of slavery was not as extensive in North Carolina as in her neighbors to the north and south, it has not been the subject of intensive research, whereas slavery in South Carolina and particularly Virginia has engaged the talents of a number of distinguished historians in recent years.

Part of this neglect may be traced to the relative paucity of manuscript sources that deal with plantation life in North Carolina as compared to Virginia, South Carolina, and Georgia where excellent sources have been preserved from both the colonial and antebellum periods. This lack of manuscript records—really personal papers, memoirs, and accounts—says much about the nature of slavery in North Carolina, for the colony was a land of small yeomen farmers who owned few, if any, slaves. Nevertheless, large slaveholders did prosper in North Carolina, particularly in the tobacco belt stretching westward from the Albemarle Sound and in the swampy lowlands of the Cape Fear. And unquestionably slavery was firmly rooted in the Old North State by 1800. But its growth lagged behind the development of slavery in other southern colony-states. Historians have usually attributed this slower rate of expansion to geography—North Carolina's ragged coastline precluded the development of good ports and its rivers retarded development of an effective road system. Thus the province's preindustrial farmers and small capitalists had to pay the higher costs of overland transportation and trade. But these are matters which primarily concerned white Carolinians.

What this study attempts to do is examine the nature of life for black Carolinians. The problem is that we catch only glimpses of most Afro-Americans through the impressions of whites. Rarely do Negroes get the chance to speak for themselves in the records. The historian's task becomes one of measuring objective black behavior against the overtly racist assumptions of most white observers. The interaction between the races was complex, and each contact between them must be milked for every possible nuance. The constant repetition of this process expands seemingly limited sources and unlocks new treasure chests of evidence.

Readers will consequently find that Afro-Americans were active, not passive, beings who in the face of unremitting adversity struggled to maintain their dignity, their African heritage, and even their lives, for the violent and brutalizing aspects of slavery obtained in North Carolina as elsewhere. They were, moreover, rational men and women who from necessity had to weigh the impact of each and every action they made. The slightest misstep in racial etiquette and expected behavior could bring whipping or mutilation.

For blacks, then, the fight for liberty associated with the American Revolution took place in a more ambiguous context than for whites. While many Negroes joined the patriot side, many more allied with the British who openly courted a black rebellion in the South and enticed slaves with promises of freedom. The hundreds of black Carolinians who followed the redcoated columns in the southern campaign of 1780-1782 or swam to the British fleet off the Cape Fear in 1776 attest to the magnitude of black longings for freedom. If the fear of servile insurrection preoccupied the minds of white Carolinians, the hope for freedom captivated the hearts of their slaves.

ACKNOWLEDGMENTS

In undertaking a study of this scope, one inevitably accumulates numerous debts from colleagues and friends who offer their encouragement and wisdom. The staffs of the State Archives and State Library patiently filled my requests and drew my attention to many arcane documents; Lee Albright, librarian for the Genealogy Section, in particular helped me track down black soldiers as did George Stevenson of the State Archives and Thomas C. Parramore of Meredith College. Robert Cain and Barbara Cain shared with me their unparalleled knowledge of the British Records and led me to many excellent sources. Robert M. Calhoon and especially Marvin L. Michael Kay and Lorin Lee Cary unselfishly offered the fruits of their research; the latter two historians are presently completing a monograph on North Carolina slavery, 1748-1772. William S. Price, Jr., Paul D. Escott, Alan D. Watson, and John Easterly read the manuscript critically. Their criticisms and strong disagreements at some points informed each page of this study. Any errors or unorthodox interpretations, of course, remain my own. The research and writing of this pamphlet were completed while Memory F. Mitchell served as administrator of the Historical Publications Section; her patience was much appreciated. Henri T. Dawkins typed the final manuscript with diligence and care, and Nancy Pentecost helped with the proofreading. Finally, the administration of the Department of Cultural Resources and Larry E. Tise, former director of the Division of Archives and History and the person who conceived the Bicentennial Pamphlet Series, proved ever supportive of this project and made its implementation possible.

Tell them that if I am Black I am free born American & a revolutionary soldier & therefore ought not to be thrown intirely out of the scale of notice.

—John Chavis to Willie P. Mangum
March 10, 1832

CHAPTER I

"To Rayse a Plantacon":
The Growth of Slavery in North Carolina

Wedged between the burgeoning tobacco plantations of Virginia and the swampy rice plantations of South Carolina, the small farms of colonial North Carolina stretched from the hazardous sand bars of the Atlantic Ocean to the foothills of the Appalachian Mountains. Carved out of thick forests of loblolly pine, these farms often bordered North Carolina's many navigable rivers, but these waterways emptied into the impoundments of the Outer Banks or flowed on into South Carolina before reaching the sea. Thus, in colonial America where mercantile interests often depended on the ease and access of ocean-going trade, North Carolina stood at a marked disadvantage.

Handicapped by its dangerous coast and lack of good harbors, North Carolina never developed the extensive slaveholding planter class that thrived in neighboring Virginia and South Carolina. Governor George Burrington succinctly stated the problem in a report to the Lords of Trade and Plantations in 1733: "Great is the loss this Country has sustained in not being supply'd by vessels from Guinea with Negroes; in any part of the Province the people are able to pay for a ships load; but as none come directly from Affrica, we are under a necessity to buy, the refuse refractory and distemper'd Negroes, brought from other Governments; It is hoped some Merchants in England will speedily furnish this Colony with Negroes, to increase the Produce and its Trade to England."[1] To infer, however, that slavery did not flourish in North Carolina is to ignore its steady growth throughout the colonial and Revolutionary period and its increasing importance to the economy and society of the colony. If North Carolina approached Thomas Jefferson's dream of an agrarian republic of small yeomen farmers, it also contained within it the seeds of another society—one based on human servitude.

There never really had been any doubt about the introduction of slavery into North Carolina. Winthrop D. Jordan has characterized the decision to enslave Negroes in seventeenth-century America as "unthinking."[2] But no such blundering seems to have affected the minds of the men who planted a colony in Carolina.

Soon after his restoration to the English throne in 1660, Charles II granted a tract of territory south of Virginia to eight Lords Proprietors. Their motives were frankly commercial. The proprietors expected to reap quick profits by renting lands and selling a wide range of commodities. No strangers to Negro servitude, the proprietors recognized that a slave colony in Carolina would enhance their commercial interests.[3]

Pressed by a group of Barbadian colonists wishing to settle in Carolina, the proprietors quickly instituted and expanded the headright system. Under that system the heads of every household were allotted acreage on the basis of the numbers of people they brought with them. Bowing to the demands of the Barbadians, the proprietors granted "the Owner of every Negro-Man or Slave, brought thither to settle within the first year, twenty acres, and for every Woman-Negro or Slave, ten acres of Land; and all Men Negro's, or slaves after that time, and within the first five years, ten acres, and for every Woman-Negro or slave, five acres." These allotments were later increased.[4]

Though some imprecision in language about "slaves" and "servants" continued to exist in seventeenth-century England, distinctive roles for Negroes were clearly evident in Carolina from its first settlement. The status of the Negro was explicitly stated in Carolina's Fundamental Constitutions, drafted in 1669 for the proprietors possibly with the assistance of political theorist John Locke. The Fundamental Constitutions represented an elaborate articulation of political philosophy and specific instructions. Article 110 asserted that, "Every freeman of Carolina, shall have absolute power and authority over his negro slaves, of what opinion or religion soever."[5] The Fundamental Constitutions also permitted slaves religious toleration but noted further that any slave converting to a Christian denomination remained in servitude.

Taken in concert, the headright system and the Fundamental Constitutions were a victory for the Barbadians whose major holdings were in slaves and who could now count on large land-holdings by settling in Carolina. But while slavery expanded rapidly in South Carolina, the institution's growth in North Carolina was more measured. Still the proprietors persisted. When one proprietor attempted to purchase sows for the settlement at Albemarle, he candidly declared his intentions: "we may have a quantity of Hoggs flesh wch will soonest come to bare to send to Barbados wch will p[ro]duce us Neagroes & Sarv^{ts}: to

This depiction of Africans landing at Jamestown, Virginia, in 1619 appeared originally in *Harper's Weekly* (January, 1901).

rayse a plantacon."[6] Lacking slaves, however, plantations were slow to develop in North Carolina.

Measuring how fast slavery grew is difficult. Population figures for blacks before 1790 are sketchy at best. Most slaves before 1730 were in the tobacco-growing region in the colony's northeastern area. In 1710 a total of 308 Negroes and 1,871 whites was reported to live in Pasquotank and Currituck counties. The number of blacks in the whole colony was estimated in 1712 at only 800.[7] By comparison South Carolina had an estimated 4,100 Negro slaves (approximately one-half the colony's total population) in 1708 and over 18,000 (nearly three times the free population) by 1720.[8] After 1730, however, slavery increased precipitously in North Carolina with the establishment of rice-growing and the naval stores industry. Historians Marvin L. Michael Kay and Lorin Lee Cary, using estimates based on black taxables (defined by the General Assembly in 1715 as all slaves over twelve years of age), have determined that between 1730 and 1767 the black population increased rapidly from 6,000 to 39,483. This dramatic growth, as much as 6 percent annually between 1755 and 1767, could not have occurred from natural increase alone but must have represented a surge in slave imports. Kay and Cary calculate, moreover, that sex ratios of black males to black females had stabilized by the 1770s at around 120 to 100, thereby allowing slaves, despite other overwhelming difficulties, to form marital and familial patterns. By 1790 the first federal census recorded 100,572 slaves and 288,204 whites in North Carolina.

By the mid-eighteenth century slaveholding patterns had assumed discernible characteristics. The size of slaveholdings in the western portion of the colony remained relatively insignificant. Only about 10 percent of the households in Orange County (1755) and Anson County (1763) held slaves, and those that did had relatively few. In the Lower Cape Fear on the other hand slaves were more widely held and in larger numbers. That area had been settled during the 1720s by planters from South Carolina who were familiar with rice culture and the uses of slave labor. In the northeast around the Albemarle Sound still another pattern emerged: the extent of households owning slaves was about the same as the Lower Cape Fear, but the number of slaves per slave-owning household was much lower. For instance, in Chowan County in 1766 about 52 percent of the households owned slaves, while in New Hanover County in 1763 the figure approached 55 percent.[9]

During the 1750s and 1760s no major changes in the distri-

4

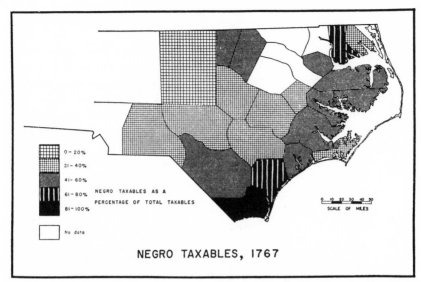

bution of slave taxables occurred, but there was a slight increase in the proportion of slave taxables. This trend was most pronounced in New Hanover County where the actual proportion of households possessing slaves decreased at the same time the absolute number of slave taxables was growing. In other words, slaveholders who already owned slaves were buying more. Thus on the eve of the American Revolution, three tendencies in North Carolina slaveholding were becoming evident. First, the slave population was growing rapidly. This in part was due to natural increase, but slaveholders were also purchasing increasing numbers. Second, the proportion of the total free population using slave labor was declining as slaveholding became more concentrated in fewer hands. Finally, an increasing segment of the slaveholders was employing large rather than small numbers of slaves.[10]

The distribution of slaves followed agricultural patterns. Slavery expanded westward from the Albemarle region with the tobacco culture through a northern tier of counties. Northampton, Halifax, and Warren counties all had large Negro populations. About 40 to 60 percent of the households in tobacco-producing areas owned slaves. But the tobacco market was volatile and thus tended to discourage large slaveholding. Similarly, farther west

5

wheat was the principal cash crop, and slavery was not necessary for its relatively easy cultivation. Slavery, however, was especially advantageous to the naval stores industry of the Lower Cape Fear where slave labor could be used efficiently during most of the year making tar, pitch, and turpentine. Rice cultivation required the largest and most skilled labor force, but it was confined to a small area of the Cape Fear, perhaps no more than 500 acres in all. The export high of rice was reached in 1771, and over 95 percent of the crop cleared the port of Brunswick. Clearly few men planted rice, and they invariably were large slaveholders in areas where the black population was heaviest. The Eagles family, for example, owned rice mills, indigo works, and lumber mills and held seventy slaves in 1775. Still, compared to South Carolina, there were few large slaveholders and large-scale planters in North Carolina. Thus while only 31 percent of the families in North Carolina held slaves in 1790, the concentration of slaveholders and slaves appeared in counties where tobacco, rice, and naval stores prospered. Both Warren and New Hanover counties, for instance, averaged 10.3 slaves per slaveholding family, while Halifax ranked next with 8.7. Randolph County, on the other hand, averaged only 3.5.[11]

William Tryon, who assumed the royal governorship in 1765, provided a revealing, if exaggerated, account of slavery in North Carolina shortly after arriving in the colony. "The Calculation of the Inhabitants in this Province," he wrote, "is one hundred and twenty Thousand White & Black of which there is a great Majority of White People. The Negroes are very numerous I suppose five to one White Person[s] in the Maritime Counties, but as you penetrate into the Country few Blacks are employed. . . ." He attributed the lack of slaves in the backcountry to the poverty of the settlers who could not afford slaves.[12] At least one Moravian observer agreed with the royal governor. According to F. W. Marshall's report from Wachovia in 1770, it was unprofitable to undertake a large estate if it was more than a family could work. "Under such circumstances," the report stated, "other people buy slaves, but to purchase ten or twelve would require an outlay of more than £ 1000: (the one we have cost £ 120: and was considered cheap), and not many of our Brethren or Sisters have the gift of handling slaves, without spoiling them."[13] The Moravian's analysis conformed closely with Tryon's estimate that slaveholders in the backcountry seldom owned more than three to ten slaves. On the other hand, Tryon continued, "in the Counties on the Sea Coast Planters have from fifty to 250 Slaves. A Plantation with

6

Seventy Slaves on it, is esteemed a good property. When a man marries his Daughters he never talks of the fortune in Money but 20 30 or 40 Slaves. . . ."[14]

Tryon made one other important observation. Slaves in North Carolina were doing every type of labor imaginable and doing it well. While blacks were employed chiefly "in the Woods & Field, Sowing, and attending and gathering in the Corn," they also made "Barrels, Hoops, Staves, Shingles, Rails, Posts and Pails, all which they do to admiration . . . ."[15] Earlier in the century John Urmston, an Anglican missionary, marveled at the "great numbers of slaves who understand most handycrafts . . . ."[16] Black carpenters, wheelwrights, coopers, butchers, tanners, shoemakers, sailors, and pilots abounded in the economy of the Carolinas. When two Virginians spent the day at the Moravian settlements in piedmont North Carolina, they were fascinated by the orderly and prosperous community. One Moravian recorded, "they asked how many negroes we had. Answer, two. They were the more surprised to find that white people had done so much work."[17]

Implicit in the Virginians' amazement was the assumption that Negroes customarily did "so much work," not whites. But white attitudes toward Negro labor in the colonial as well as antebellum South remained naggingly ambivalent. Johann David Schoepf, a stern teutonic traveler, complained about an enforced four-day stay in Edenton because no ferry was available to cross the Albemarle Sound. The ferryman had given the boat to the Negroes for a holiday. "No people can be so greedy after holidays," he decided, "as the whites and blacks here, and none with less reason, for at no time do they work so as to need a long rest. It is difficult to say which are the best creatures, the whites here or their blacks, or which have been formed by the others; but in either case the example is bad. The white men are all the time complaining that the blacks will not work, and they themselves do nothing. The white men complain further that they cannot trust the faithless blacks, and they set them a dubious model." At a tavern, the sardonic German observed: "Here was much a-do about nothing, half a dozen negroes were running about the house all day, and nothing was attended to, unless one saw to it himself."[18]

Planters, naturally, groused most about the work habits of their slaves. Charles Pettigrew delayed a trip to town because he found it "disagreeable to leave everything to the management of careless negroes . . . ." On another occasion, Pettigrew, who owned one of the larger plantations in eastern North Carolina on Lake Phelps, returned home and found that "the negroes had been cutting Rice almost all the week." But in his view the slaves had "done just nothing from the time I had left them last. The fodder hangs all dead on the stalks except about a couple of cart loads of Blades." Nor did Pettigrew like his overseer who seemed "to be as much of a negro in principle as is a one of them . . . ." The irate planter believed that "overseers require little less oversight from their imployers than the negroes require from *them*, & that in point of *fidelity*, there is not so much *Difference* between *white* & *black* as our natural partiality for the former would persuade us."[19]

Yet slave labor was unquestionably productive, and Negroes performed ably if not steadily despite the complaints of their masters. Even Pettigrew recognized what historian Eugene D. Genovese has since termed the "black work ethic."[20] Blacks resisted the excesses of an oppressive labor system which demanded routinized work and the discipline of regularity, but they could not escape (except literally) or shirk the hard work endemic to all colonial society. The work on a plantation in particular had its own rhythm, coming in spurts at various times of the year. Harvest time demanded hard and diligent labor. Slaves and masters ultimately achieved a balance between expectations and objectives; it was a mutual process in which each side, as in any labor system, managed to define in varying degrees its limits and its role. Pettigrew ultimately fired his overseers with salutary results: "We have no Overseer, choosing rather to oversee the negroes, than an Overseer & them too . . . . The negroes at the Lake plantation have commonly done better by themselves with a little direction than with such overseers as we have had."[21]

Negroes, then, formed a crucial segment of the vanguard of pioneers who cleared the land and settled America. The work was harsh. To cultivate rice, for instance, required an enormous expenditure of labor. Cypress and gum forests had to be cut, and the rice fields were continually obstructed by logs and stumps. A minimum of thirty slaves was needed to work a rice plantation, and in North Carolina there were only twenty or so planters on the Lower Cape Fear in the colonial period who could mobilize such a work force at a time when naval stores returned a quicker and healthier profit. The system depended to a large extent on hand labor. Janet Schaw, a Scottish gentlewoman, provided a vivid description of the rice culture in the Lower Cape Fear in 1775: "The rice too is whitening, and its distant appearance is that of our green oats, but there is no living near it with the putrid

water that must lie on it, and the labour required for it is only fit
for slaves, and I think the hardest work I have seen them engaged
in."[22] Each slave was expected to produce four or five barrels of
rice averaging 500 pounds each—the equivalent of two acres'
produce. Black hands broke the soil with a hoe, sowed the seeds
from a gourd, cut the ripened crop with a sickle, flailed the rice for
threshing, and polished the white grains with a mortar and
pestle.[23]

Various aspects of rice cultivation on the Cape Fear River were depicted
in these sketches by James E. Taylor, published in *Frank Leslie's Illustrated
Newspaper* (October 20, 1866).

The tasks were laborious and demanded more than mere menial
labor. As historian Peter Wood has perceptively suggested, skills
acquired in Africa contributed in no small measure to the success
of rice-growing in the Carolinas. Indeed, the competence of
Africans with respect to rice cultivation may have been a principal
attraction for the English colonists and led to the rapid importa-
tion of slaves during the eighteenth century. Negroes from the
West Coast of Africa were noted rice farmers who sold the white

grain to Portuguese, French, and English explorers and slave traders. One white observer insisted that rice formed the chief part of the West Africans' sustenance.[24]

The techniques utilized to cultivate the crop in the Carolinas were little different from those employed in Africa. New World slaves planted the crop in the spring by making a hole with the heel and covering the seeds with the foot. In the summer Carolina blacks formed rows to move through the rice fields with their hoes, working and singing in unison. The flat winnowing baskets used to fan the threshed rice in the wind bore African designs and were crafted by African hands. Negroes also supplied the most efficient means of "cleaning" the rice crop despite European and American attempts to devise a better method. Several blacks, normally women, placed small amounts of the grain in a wooden mortar and beat the rice with long wooden pestles which had a sharp edge at one end to separate the husks and a flat tip at the other to whiten the grain. Faced with the stringent food rationing slaveholders usually imposed on blacks and encouraged to raise their own subsistence, Negroes from West Africa doubtless nurtured the white grain where their masters had failed and thereby introduced and sustained one of the South's most important staple crops in the colonial period.[25]

NORTH CAROLINA

The naval stores industry of the Lower Cape Fear continued to be a profitable enterprise long after the colonial period, as shown here in a nineteenth-century drawing from *Harper's Weekly*.

If the cultivation of rice was backbreaking and tied to hand labor, agricultural techniques for other North Carolina crops were hardly more advanced. Janet Schaw was astonished to find the stalks of last year's crops still in the ground. Nor were the fields plowed: "the only instrument used is a hoe, with which they at once till and plant corn. To accomplish this a number of Negroes follow each other's tail the day long, and have a task assigned them, and it will take twenty at least to do as much work as two horses with a man and a boy would perform."[26] Even so, North Carolina blacks, according to John Brickell, one of the colony's earliest historians, were "very industrious and laborious in improving their Plantations, planting abundance of *Corn, Rice* and *Tobacco* and making vast Quantities of *Turpentine, Tar,* and *Pitch,* being better able to undergo fatigues in the extremity of the hot Weather than any *Europeans.*"[27]

The naval stores industry to which Brickell alluded was ideally suited to the use of slave labor. Slaves "boxed" a pine tree by cutting large cavities in it. This procedure caused turpentine to flow which the slaves then ladled into barrels. According to Johann Schoepf, "One man can readily care for 3000 boxes, and that number is generally assigned one negro, the negroes doing the most of this work. At the best and warmest season one negro can easily fill 15-20 barrels of turpentine a day."[28]

Pine trees "ran" for about three years before falling to the ground. Known now as lightwood, the trees were gathered up by slaves for the purpose of making tar and pitch. During the winter months the slaves collected "great quantities of this *Light-wood*" which was cut up and burned in kilns to produce the tar and pitch. The kilns had to be tended "Night and Day" until they burned out, a process which might take up to forty hours. "It sometimes happens," Brickell wrote, "through ill management, and especially in too dry Weather, that these Kilns are blown up as if a train of Gunpowder had been laid under them by which Accident their *Negroes* have been very much burnt or scalded." Few white men, in Brickell's view, matched the Negroes "in hard labour."[29]

Black women rarely received preferential treatment. Their labor was considered as valuable as the men's, and so they were counted among the taxables, though white women were not. "The female slaves," noted one traveler, "fare, labour, and repose, just in the same manner; even when they breed, which is generally every two or three years, they seldom lose more than a week's work thereby, either in the delivery, or suckling the child."[30]

Negro craftsmen were doubly valuable. Masters could utilize their talents at home or hire them out to another slaveholder, usually for a term of one year. "There are several *Blacks* born here that can Read and Write," Brickell reported, "others that are bred to Trades, and prove good Artists."[31] An advertisement in the *North Carolina Gazette* in 1778 offered three such skilled slaves: "To be sold for ready money, two likely young negro fellows, the one a very good cooper, the other a good sailor, and has also been used to plantation work. Likewise a house wench, who is a tolerable good cook, and can wash, iron, spin and weave."[32] Negro artisans frequently worked in the colony's ports. The list of caulkers who repaired the HMS *Scorpion* off the Cape Fear in 1751 included Jack, Andrew, Minalaus, Pompey, Santee, Newborn, and Phillip.[33] Planters were always interested in finding productive and profitable work for their slaves. When William Blount served as a North Carolina delegate to the Constitutional Convention in Philadelphia in 1787, he noticed the employment of Negroes there as nail makers. He wrote his brother: "your man Pollypus and my man Will I suppose would readily make as good Nails as any body and I have four boys the greater part of which you Know I talked of making Coopers who I suppose would as readily learn as the White boys I have seen here. . . ."[34]

Thus, blacks performed complex and essential tasks in North Carolina's economy and society. If their status often forced them into menial labor, they still contributed skills and know-how to the colony's agriculture and crafts. It seems doubtful, however, that North Carolina slaves received in return for their labor anything approaching an equivalent value in shelter, clothing, and food, as Robert W. Fogel and Stanley L. Engerman have recently argued about slavery as a whole.[35] By all accounts, North Carolina blacks in the colonial period were ill-fed, ill-housed, and ill-clothed. In a frontier society, privation and harsh living conditions were common to all, but in the case of slaves these conditions proved especially acute.

North Carolina blacks received minimal support from planters. Guardians for orphaned children, for example, seldom charged more than £ 3 per year to board Negroes belonging to an orphan's estate. The cost of sheltering white children was at least twice that.[36] Johann Schoepf asserted: "The keep of a negro here does not come to a great figure, since the daily ration is but a quart of maize, and rarely a little meat or salted fish. Only those negroes kept for house-service are better cared for." The better masters gave slaves "a suit of coarse wollen cloth, two rough shirts, and a pair of shoes" once a year. Planters with the largest slaveholdings, according to Schoepf, kept blacks "the worst, let them run naked mostly or in rags, and accustom them as much as possible to hunger, but exact of them steady work."[37]

Most observers agreed with Schoepf's depiction of blacks' living conditions. A Continental officer traveling through the South in 1781 at the end of the Revolutionary War found the condition of slaves in Virginia and North Carolina appalling. "Their Negro's tho' at this Season of the year [late November] are almost Naked in General," he wrote. "Some of them Quite as Naked as they were born Have Come into our Camp to look for peices [sic] of Old Clothes.—I don't Know how they Reconcile this treatment of their Slaves with their Liberal Principles of Hospitality.—When Such a trifle of Expence would give them some Kind of Coarse Clothing to Cover their Nakedness."[38] Another traveler "saw a Negroe in only his shirt bringing a horse from the fields, he shook with cold." Well he might in December, 1787. The same observer reported on another occasion, "There was playing at . . . [the] door five Negroe Children every one dress'd in a Shirt only— Clothes are not bestowed on these Animals with much profusion— At Johnson's one was Walking abot. the Court Yard absolutely naked, and in Newbern I saw a boy thro' the Street with only a Jacket on, and that unbuttoned."[39] Black women wore "a coarse Kind of Cloth wrapped around their Waists unless they are very small." Writing from New Bern in 1778, Ebenezer Hazard "saw . . . a Negro Woman with nothing on her but a very ragged Petti-coat."[40]

The slaves' diet proved as scant as their clothing. Rising at day-break to begin work in the fields, slaves often went without breakfast. In the tobacco regions, blacks built a fire next to the fields where they labored and at noon ate "homminy and salt" and less often "a little fat, skimmed milk, rusty bacon, or salt herring to relish [their] homminy, or hoecake. . . ." Work continued until evening when the slaves returned to the tobacco houses "where each has his task in stripping allotted him. . . ." Only then did they have a second meal. Each slave received one blanket for bed and covering and slept on a bench or the ground. Clothing for slaves in the tobacco belt might include a shirt and trousers in the summer, and a woollen jacket, breeches, and shoes in the winter.[41]

In the low country working conditions in the rice fields were just as severe. Elkanah Watson in 1777 "observed a large collection of negroes, seated upon rice straw, making a miserable meal upon boiled rice and pure water. It is truly astonishing, how the slave can sustain life with this wretched pittance, and even appear in good health and condition, compelled to labor from dawn to night, through the long summer days, under the scorching rays of the intense sun. . . ."[42]

Given the meager provisions they received, slaves were left to their own devices to supplement their diet. John Brickell recorded numerous types of wild game and fish the Negroes ate, but which whites disdained. Blacks esteemed possums "very much," according to Brickell, and also ate bats, turtles, owls, and other fowl which the naturalist found ill-tasting and "very hard of Digesting."[43]

But besides hunting and fishing, slaves also were permitted to cultivate their own gardens. A North Carolina slaveholder explained to William Attmore, who visited the state in the 1780s, that "the allowance of provision made to a working Slave, in a part of this State and in South Carolina, was *one peck of Indian Corn per Week*: this he was to dress or cook as he pleased; they are allowed no Meat, they have the privilege sometimes of working a bit of Ground for themselves, out of such time as they gain when Task'd, or on Sundays."[44] Janet Schaw concluded that, "The Negroes are the only people that seem to pay any attention to the various uses that wild vegetables may be put to. . . . The allowance for a Negro is a quart of Indian corn p^r day, . . . and a little piece of land which they cultivate much better than their Master. There they rear hogs and poultry, sow calabashes, etc. and are better provided for in every thing than the poorer white people with us."[45]

Having completed their assigned tasks for their master, slaves doubtless did take special care of their own plots. An industrious slave could not only improve his diet but also sell any surplus in order to purchase needed clothing or personal articles. It was not uncommon for slaves to market rice, corn, potatoes, or even tobacco. John Brickell declared that blacks used the money they earned to "buy Hats, and other Necessaries for themselves, as *Linnen, Bracelets, Ribbons*, and several other Toys for their Wives and Mistresses."[46] Slaves, however, always ran the risk of becoming too competitive with whites. In 1774, for instance, the General Assembly prohibited slaves from cultivating tobacco for their "own benefit" in Halifax, Northampton, Bute, Granville, Orange, Chatham, Edgecombe, and Wake counties.[47]

In light of the blacks' living conditions, it is not surprising that slaveholders constantly bemoaned the "indolence, thievery, and untruth" of the bondsmen.[48] Effectively stripped of most property rights and reduced to servile labor, slaves stole to keep alive and to mitigate the brutalizing aspects of their lives. Janet Schaw reported of one planter's difficulties with Negroes who "tore up his fences, [and] carried off what they could eat and destroyed the rest." "They steal whatever they can come at," Schaw declared, "and even intercept the cows and milk them. They are indeed the constant plague of their tyrants, whose severity or mildness is equally regarded by them in these Matters."[49]

Despite the seemingly narrow constraints of their lives, blacks did have time for more leisurely pursuits. Sundays and sometimes Saturday afternoons were traditionally days of rest. After a hard day's work in the fields, a slave might set out "six or seven miles" to attend a "negroe dance, in which he performs with astonishing agility, and the most vigorous exertions, keeping time and cadence, most exactly, with the music of a banjor (a large hollow instrument with three strings), and a quaqua (somewhat resembling a drum), until he exhausts himself. . . ."[50] Witnessing a funeral in North Carolina, Janet Schaw recorded: "the Negroes assembled to perform their part of the funeral rites, which they did by running, jumping, crying and various exercises. They are a noble troop, the best in all the country. . . ."[51] Negroes also shared white North Carolinians' passion for horse racing and gaming. Visiting the farm of Wright Stanly near New Bern, William Attmore keenly watched the horse races in which the "Riders were young Negroes of 13 or 14 years old who generally rode bareback." The puritanical Attmore censured the practice because of "betting; much quarreling wrangling, Anger, Swearing & drinking is created . . . I saw white Boys, and Negroes eagerly betting . . . a quart of Rum, a drink of Grog &c, as well as Gentlemen betting high—"[52]

Within the black community Negroes attempted to maintain social and familial institutions in the face of adverse pressures. A slaveholder might or might not choose to recognize a family unit or a marriage between a Negro man and woman. According to John Brickell, the slave marriages were "generally performed amongst themselves, there being very little ceremony used upon

Slaveholders often grumbled about bondsmen who spent their nights "rambling" and were too tired to work in the fields the following morning. These sketches by E. W. Kemble appeared in the *Century Magazine*, XXXI (1885-1886), 525, 808.

that Head; for the Man makes the Woman a Present, such as a *Brass Ring* or some other Toy, which if she accepts of, becomes his Wife; but if ever they part from each other, which frequently happens, upon any little Disgust, she returns his Present...." Slavery could render such marriages unstable. "It frequently happens," Brickell wrote, "when these Women have no Children by the first Husband, after being a Year or two cohabiting together, the Planters oblige them to take a second, third, fourth, fifth, or more Husbands or Bedfellows, a fruitful Woman amongst them being very much valued by the Planters, and a numerous Issue esteemed the greatest Riches in this Country." A child's status followed that of his or her mother's. If she were a slave, then her children became the property of the planter to whom she belonged. Still blacks often tried tenaciously to protect the integrity of their family life. "And though they have no other Ceremony in their Marriages," Brickell observed, "than what I have represented, yet they seem to be Jealously inclined, and fight most desperately amongst themselves when they Rival each other, which they commonly do."[53]

Herbert G. Gutman, drawing in part from the records of North Carolina plantations, has argued persuasively in his recent book on the black family that the slave families were much more stable and viable than previously thought.[54] But even the sturdiest slave marriage could not avoid the dangers and fears posed by the slave trade. Most of North Carolina's slave trade came overland from South Carolina or Virginia which inevitably meant higher prices for slaves. The colony's irascible governor, George Burrington, complained again in 1736 to the English Commissioners of Customs about North Carolina's economy suffering without the direct shipment of slaves from Guinea or the Sugar Islands. "The Planters," the governor reported, "are obliged to go into Virginia and South Carolina to purchase them where they pay a duty on each Negroe or buy the refuse distempered or refractory Negroes brought into the Country from New England and the Islands which are sold at excessive Rates."[55]

The nexus of the slave trade was the auction block which was often held under the "sheriff's hammer." The Negroes were "driven in from [the] country like swine for market."[56] Those slaves not sold outright were hired by the highest bidder. Observing an auction in Wilmington, Johann Schoepf recorded: "A whole family, man, wife, and 3 children were hired out at 70 Pd. a year; and others singly, at 25, 30, 35 Pd., according to age, strength, capability, and usefulness." By the 1780s slaves sold for £120 to £180 or roughly five to six times their annual hire. Schoepf witnessed the sale of a black cooper and his fifteen-year-old son for £250 and £150 respectively, and indeed a slave artisan normally brought a higher price. Auctioneers often made extravagant claims about the slaves, but the Negroes themselves, Schoepf mused, "contradict everything good that is said about them; complain of their age, longstanding misery or sickness, and declare that purchasers will be selling themselves in buying them ... because they know well that the dearer their cost, the more work will be required of them."[57]

The auction block represented the ultimate degradation of the Afro-American. "If negresses are put up," Schoepf asserted, "scandalous and indecent questions and jests are permitted."[58] Nothing, however, could approach the kind of misery Elkanah Watson witnessed in Wilmington in 1778: "A wench clung to a little daughter, and implored, with the most agonizing supplication, that they might not be separated." The slaves were sold to different masters.[59]

By the middle of the eighteenth century slavery was well entrenched in North Carolina. Though indentured servitude— "Christian servants" as they were known—and even Indian enslavement existed alongside Negro slavery during these years, they were clearly in decline by the time of the American Revolution. Black bondage provided a stable labor force not just for a long term but for a lifetime. As the slave system expanded, white Carolinians searched for means to insure the fixed status of the growing number of blacks and to provide for their own security against the omnipresent fear of servile insurrection.

CHAPTER II

"Lest Our Slaves Become Our Masters": Patterns of White Control

As the institution of slavery expanded in eighteenth-century North Carolina, the need to control the growing black population became a persistent problem for whites whose security and prosperity depended on Negro bondage. The Fundamental Constitutions and colonial practice had firmly fixed the Africans' status, but there were few guideposts to regulate slaves' behavior, to insure a stable work force, and to lessen inherent tensions between master and slave. A North Carolinian writing to the Commissioners of Trade in 1715 expressed the fear common to all societies based on slavery. Alarmed by suggestions that slaves in Carolina might be armed for defense against French and Spanish attacks, he warned: "there must be great Caution used, lest our Slaves when arm'd might become our Masters."[1]

Questions arising from various activities by Negroes doubtless helped prompt the first slave code in 1715 which collated and updated previous statutes. Up until that time some confusion evidently existed. In 1705, for example, a group of white Carolinians petitioned the Lords Proprietors about certain voting irregularities. Their memorial reported that "in the year 1703 when a new General Assembly was to be chosen, ... the Election was managed with very great partiality and Injustice, and all sorts of people, even servants, Negroes, Aliens, Jews and Common sailors were admitted to vote in Elections." To prevent a recurrence of such unbridled democracy, the General Assembly passed a law in 1715 stating "that no person whatsoever Inhabitant of this Government born out of the Allegiance of his Majesty and not made free no Negro Mullatto or Indians shall be capable of voting for Members of Assembly. . . ."[2]

The denial of suffrage, however, hardly compared with the coercive strictures placed on blacks by "An Act Concerning Servants and Slaves" adopted in 1715. The law attempted for the first time to define the social, economic, and even physical place of the Negro population. Blacks could not leave their "Plantations without a Ticket or White servant along with them. . . ." White Carolinians were instructed to "use their utmost endeavors to apprehend all such Servants & Slaves as they conceive to be runaways or travell without a Tickett or that shall be seen off his Master's ground Arm'd with any Gun, Sword or any other Weapon of defence. . . ." Moreover, if "any person or persons shall kill any Runaway Slave that hath lyen out two months such person or persons shall not be called to answer for the same. . . ."

Slaves were also denied access to the courts. If a slave were accused of any crime or offense, he or she was tried by three justices of the precinct court and "three Freeholders such as have Slaves" who served as judge and jury. The special six-man tribunal was empowered to issue certificates for the value of slaves who were killed while being apprehended or executed for capital crimes. Slaveholders could then lay the certificates before the General Assembly for reimbursement. The executions of Negroes were held publicly "to the Terror of other Slaves." And slaveholders paid a poll tax on all their slaves to compensate the owners of executed slaves.

To discourage miscegenation, a white indentured woman who had "a Bastard child" by a Negro, mulatto, or Indian had her term of service extended two years or paid a fine of £6 to the Anglican church wardens. Nor could she keep the child, who was bound out as an indentured servant by the church wardens until the age of thirty-one. In the same vein, the 1715 statute ordered that "no White man or woman shall intermarry with any Negro, Mulatto or Indyan Man or Woman under the penalty of Fifty Pounds for each White man or woman." Clerics and magistrates likewise could not "celebrate such a marriage."

The lawmakers also frowned upon manumission. No owner was permitted to free "Runaway or Refractory Negroes," but those who had performed "honest & Faithful service" could be emancipated. Freed slaves, however, must leave the province within six months or be sold back into slavery for five years.

Always suspicious of slave gatherings, white Carolinians in the 1715 slave code prohibited any Negro "Meeting House upon the Acct. of Worship or upon any pretence." This particular restriction came at a time when Anglican missionaries were already complaining that slaveholders refused to permit the baptism of their slaves for fear that the bondsmen would then become free.[3]

Enforcing the slave code became the responsibility of whites in general but slaveholders in particular. John Brickell astutely discerned both the legal and extralegal means of imposing white control over the black population. Some slaveholders wielded the whip to maintain discipline and order. "I have frequently seen them [Negroes] whipt to that degree," Brickell said, "that large pieces of their Skin have been hanging down their Backs; yet I never observed one of them shed a Tear, which plainly shews them to be a People of very harsh and stubborn Dispositions." Other slaveholders sometimes devised ingenious forms of punishment. Tobacco planters forced their slaves to eat tobacco worms "when they have been negligent in their Tobacco Fields, and have not carefully gathered them from amongst the Tobacco Leaves . . . ." Habitual runaway slaves and servants were compelled to "have Neckyoaks put on them, which they constantly wear. . . ."[4]

Virtually shorn of any legal rights in colonial North Carolina, slaves were expected to conform to strict standards of behavior as determined by the white population. Noting the laws enacted to keep blacks "in Subjection," Brickell described how summary justice was dispensed in eighteenth-century North Carolina: "if a *Negroe* cut or wound his Master or a Christian with any unlawful Weapon, such as a *Sword, Scymiter*, or even a *Knife*, and there is Blood-shed, [and] if it is known amongst the Planters, they immediately meet and order him to be hanged, which is always performed by another Negroe, and generally the Planters bring most of their Negroes with them to behold their fellow Negroe suffer, to deter them from the like vile Practice." Brickell contended that such stern methods were necessary to prevent slave insurrections.[5]

If the slave code and social sanctions provided swift and arbitrary punishment, they often failed to meet every contingency or completely suppress black initiatives. That the laws were not always effective is documented in the many amendments and revisions which were enacted after 1715 and before the Revolution. In 1723 the General Assembly was forced to pass an act in response to complaints "of great Numbers of Free Negroes, Mulattoes, and other persons of mixt Blood, that have lately removed themselves into this Government, and that several of them have intermarried with the white Inhabitants of this Province. . . ." The law therefore redefined taxables as all males and females over twelve years of age whether free Negroes or mulattoes who traced their African ancestry as far back as three generations. Moreover, any white person marrying a Negro, mulatto, or mustee was subject to the same tax. Finally, because many freed slaves were not leaving the province within six months of their manumission as required by the 1715 law, the penalty was extended to reenslavement for seven years instead of five.[6]

By 1741 when the most elaborate slave code in colonial North Carolina was drafted, the rapid growth of the black population clearly demanded extraordinary security measures to protect white lives and investments. Any sign of slave disgruntlement or departure from accepted social norms was taken as evidence of a possible rebellion. The slightest assertion of independence or individuality by a slave could be interpreted as insolence. South Carolina, whose black population was twice that of the whites', had narrowly escaped a racial cataclysm in 1739 when a band of slaves revolted some twenty miles from Charlestown on the Stono River. And that scare had sent tremors through North Carolina.

The 1741 statute "Concerning Servants and Slaves" demonstrated the types of black initiatives which disquieted the white community. Whites were barred from trading or selling with slaves or servants unless consent had been given by their masters. Similarly, slaves were prohibited from raising horses, cattle, or hogs for their own benefit. The law stated, moreover, that no slave "shall go armed with Gun, Sword, Club or other Weapon, or shall keep any such Weapon, or shall Hunt or Range in the Woods" unless carrying a certificate from his master. Offending slaves were to receive twenty lashes, and the master had to deliver in writing to the county court the names of all Negroes who used arms, slaves "wearing Liveries always excepted."

Rewards were also instituted for the return of runaways. If a slave could not "speak English, or through Obstinacy, will not declare the name of his or her Owner," then the Negro was to be kept in jail by the county sheriff for two months during which time the official was to advertise the slave's whereabouts. If not claimed, the slave was shipped from constable to constable across the province until finally being hired out by the province with "an iron Collar to be put on the Neck of such Negro or Runaway with the letters P. G. stamped thereon [Public Gaol] . . . ." Each constable was permitted to administer thirty-nine lashes on the runaways as they were shuttled from county to county. "And whereas many Times Slaves run away and lie out and hid and lurking in the Swamps, Woods and other Obscure Places, killing Cattle and Hogs, and committing other Injuries," magistrates were empowered to issue proclamations against such slaves requiring them to surrender. If the slaves failed to return immediately, "it shall be lawful for any Person or Persons whatsoever to kill and destroy" the slaves by any means without accusation of any crime.

To prevent slave insurrections, the 1741 act declared that if three or more slaves were found guilty of conspiring "to rebell, or make insurrection" they were to be put to death. Three justices and four slave-owning freeholders were to constitute a tribunal to try "all Manner of Crimes and Offences that shall be committed by any Slave or Slaves . . . ." If any Negro, mulatto, or Indian— bond or free—who was not a Christian gave false testimony before the county court at such trials, he was straightway—without trial—"to have one Ear nailed to the Pillory, and there stand for the Space of One Hour, and the said Ear to be cut off, and thereafter the other Ear nailed in a like manner, and cut off, at the Expiration of one other Hour"; then he was to receive thirty-nine lashes "well laid on." In such instances wherein a slave was executed, slaveholders were again allowed to submit claims for compensation to the General Assembly.

The 1741 slave code made it illegal for anyone to import as a slave a Negro who was "free in any Christian country" and compelled the offender to return the black to his or her original home. But the manumission of slaves was made exceedingly difficult. The act ordered that no "Negro or Mulatto Slaves shall be set free, upon any Pretence whatsoever, except for meritorious Services, to be adjudged and allowed of by the County Court. . . ." And emancipated blacks were still required to leave the province within six months or be sold back into slavery.[7] John Brickell shrewdly observed: "The Planters seeing the Inconveniencies that might attend these kind of Priviledges to the *Negroes* [manumission], have this and all other Laws against them continually put in practice, to prevent all Opportunities they might lay hold of to make themselves formidable."[8]

Throughout the colonial period, as Brickell noted, slaveholders amended or revised the slave code to protect their interests. In 1753 an additional act on slaves and servants declared that the 1741 statute had "proved ineffectual to restrain many slaves in divers parts of this province from going armed, which may prove of dangerous consequences." Under the new law masters must post a bond for all blacks who carried arms. In addition slave patrols were appointed to examine Negroes' quarters for weapons at least four times a year.[9]

Occasionally authorities in Great Britain attempted to ameliorate the harsh justice meted out in North Carolina. In the 1730s and again in the 1750s the king instructed the colony's royal governors to enact a law "for the restraining of any inhuman

Armed slaves were a constant source of concern for southern whites. Increasingly strict laws were imposed during the eighteenth century to limit the number of slaves who could hunt and thus bear arms. Kemble sketch from the *Century Magazine*, **XXXI** (1885-1886), 822.

severity which by ill masters or their overseers may be used towards their Christian servants and their slaves, and that provision be made therein that the willfull killing of Indians and negroes may be punished with death, and that a fit penalty be imposed for the maiming of them."[10] Governor Arthur Dobbs introduced such a bill to the General Assembly in 1755, but it did not pass. In 1773 William Hooper, a whig lawyer then in the forefront of the Revolutionary movement, drafted a bill which made the murder of a slave equivalent to the murder of a freeman. The bill passed both houses, but royal Governor Josiah Martin, doubtless piqued by his other conflicts with the radical whigs, rejected it. However, in 1774 the bill passed, the governor acquiesced, and it finally became a crime to kill a slave in North Carolina, unless the murdered Negro had tried to defend himself.[11]

North Carolina's system of justice for blacks had other curious features. During the French and Indian War black male offenders were castrated instead of executed. The compensation of slaveholders for executed slaves, first codified in 1715 and again in 1741, had cost the province an increasing amount of money as the black population and slave prices rose. As John Brickell wrote in 1737: "the Planters suffer little or nothing by it [slave executions], for the Province is obliged to pay the full value they judge them worth to the Owner . . . to prevent the Planters being ruined by the loss of their Slaves, whom they have purchased at so dear a rate. . . ."[12]

In 1758 the assembly enacted a law which lasted for the remainder of the French and Indian War. The statute first of all refused compensation to all slaveholders whose slaves committed crimes while hired out. This provision also applied to any imported slaves who had been transported to North Carolina for previous crimes. But then the lawmakers ruled that no male slave condemned to death for a first offense, with the exception of murder or rape, should be executed but should rather "suffer castration." Sheriffs were authorized to administer the penalty, and the amount of compensation to any slaveholder whose slave was executed was set at £60.[13]

Most colonies outside of New England did provide compensation for executed slaves. In North Carolina the compensation was awarded by the Committee of Claims in the General Assembly with the approval of the governor. The provincial taxes of all the counties, even those with few slaves, financed the compensations.

In a recent study of this compensation practice, historians

Marvin L. Michael Kay and Lorin Lee Cary have argued that the grisly substitution of castration for execution was attributable to the financial pressures brought on by the French and Indian War. As the costs of war and higher taxes squeezed the financial resources of the colony, so did compensation claims which had mushroomed. The 1758 law was in force for five years, and it did reduce the provincial outlay for compensations. However, the decline in executions was offset by a precipitous rise in castrations—sixteen for the period 1759-1764. Moreover, slave prices continually rose during the 1750s and 1760s, so that when a 1764 act repealed the practice of castration it still raised the compensation limit for slave owners to £80. Fiscal pressures of war, of course, had relaxed by 1764, but perhaps slaveholders also preferred to replace recalcitrant male slaves out of public revenues than continue to deal with them after castration. Only two castrations occurred between 1765 and 1772, but executions quadrupled to fifty-two. Slave compensations were no incidental expense to the colony. For the period 1748 to 1772, slave compensations accounted for about 21 to 25 percent of all claims, excluding remunerations to members and officials of the assembly.[14]

The American Revolution did not end the practice of compensating slaveholders for executed slaves. In 1779 the legislature fixed a maximum value for an executed slave at £700 in continental money. But in 1786 all such laws were repealed since "many persons by cruel treatment of their slaves cause them to commit crimes for which many of the said slaves are executed." Because the burden of paying for executed slaves fell on the whole state and was therefore considered unfair by counties with few slaves, the General Assembly in 1796 authorized seven eastern counties to impose taxes to pay for executed slaves within their respective borders. Under that law a slaveholder received only two-thirds of the value of the slave as estimated by the court which convicted the offender.[15]

Punishment of whites in colonial North Carolina was severe as well, but it did not compare with the painful and merciless measures taken against blacks. No whites were legally castrated while nineteen blacks were. White offenders were sometimes branded on the thumb, hanged for a capital crime, or whipped, but they invariably received fewer lashes. In a society where minor transgressions or the act of running away could bring a death sentence, blacks knew a terror which white Carolinians could hardly comprehend.

If white control of blacks had an Achilles heel, it was nowhere more evident than in North Carolina's towns, especially those on the colony's waterways. Though less than 5 percent of North Carolina's white population lived in its urban areas, the prevalence of slaves in the towns generated anxieties and unique problems for whites which were not so pronounced in a rural setting. In an urban environment the normal restraints on slaves broke down, and black bondsmen achieved an autonomy rarely possible on a plantation. With so many slaves working in the markets, on the docks, and mingling with free blacks the slaveholders' scrutiny was diminished if not obscured. Charles Pettigrew recognized the allures of town life for blacks. When his slave Pompey ran off, Pettigrew suspected that he had gone to Edenton to make his way north. "I am sorry, I had occasion to take him to Town lately," the slave owner moaned, "as he had opportunity to hear of so many [slaves] getting off so easily from there." Similarly, Ebenezer Pettigrew later urged the reinstitution of a night guard in Edenton as "useful & necessary" since the blacks were too "numerous there to have uncurbed liberty at night, night is their day."[16]

The regulations adopted to control slave behavior once again reflected the types of black initiatives which corroded the institution of slavery. As early as 1745 the General Assembly empowered the Wilmington town commissioners to monitor the role of slaves in the markets. Henceforth slaves had to have a ticket from their masters to sell produce; the measure was deemed necessary to prevent "all Irregular Mobbs & Caballs by Negroes and others . . . ."[17]

The activities of slaves in the marketplace proved especially vexing to the slaveholders, for the black tradesmen could sell their wares, produce, or crafts without the master's vigilant eye. Slaves could thereby keep all or part of the money they earned rather than turn it over entirely to their masters. Some masters, to be sure, permitted their slaves to keep part of the earnings for subsistence and housing. But the overall situation invited too many abuses, in the eyes of whites, and demonstrably tattered the fabric of slavery. In town, away from the slaveholders' supervision, slaves simply had too much independence. William Hooper, the Revolutionary leader, groused in 1773 that his slaves were selling everything they could pillage from his home in Wilmington or nearby plantation.[18] Even the Moravians had cause for complaint.

The minutes of the Salem Boards in 1774 declared: "As there is much illicit buying and selling being done by negroes, to the disturbance of the Congregation . . . no one should buy from such a person unless he could show a permit from his master. In general there should be less conversation with the negroes, as that naturally has no good result."[19]

To regulate urban slaves, then, the Wilmington commissioners in 1765 enacted a set of strict ordinances. Negroes marketing various commodities in the town were required to have a ticket from their masters stating the slaves' names and business. Authorities could seize any slave not holding such a ticket. Furthermore, anyone who bartered with Negroes not having a ticket was subject to a fine of thirty-five shillings.

Since masters frequently allowed slaves to find work for themselves in the town and then arrange their own lodging, the Wilmington ordinances ruled that slaves could not "hire any House" or "go at large, [to] hire him, her or themselves out for any longer than day to day. . . ." Until then slaves often paid rents for their own houses on a weekly or even longer basis "which tend[s] greatly to promote Idleness, Revelling and disturbance, Thievery and Stealing and many other crimes. . . ." Nor could Wilmington citizens rent a house or tenement to slaves any longer. If a Negro were hired out, the person getting the slave's services had to write tickets specifying the slave's name and business. And the master was to receive all the slave's wages directly. Slaves offering themselves for hire without a ticket could be whipped or jailed for twenty-four hours. Similarly, all blacks performing "any Trade, mistery or Occupation" must be under the direction of some "white person."

Finally, Wilmington's 1765 ordinances "for the better regulation of Negroes and other slaves" prohibited any number of blacks over three from gathering in "Streets, alleys, Vacant Lots," or houses for the purpose of "playing, Riotting, Caballing." To insure compliance a curfew on slaves was set at 10 o'clock each night. Slaves out after curfew had to carry a ticket and candle.[20]

Though it does not appear from the evidence that Wilmington Negroes monopolized parts of the local market as blacks in Charlestown a short distance south did, they proved a troublesome property. Wilmington's ordinances failed to limit the slaves' inordinate freedom in the urban setting. In 1772 the commissioners were forced to order that "all Slaves who keep Houses seperate [sic] from their Master or Mistress, do remove by the first day of March next, under the penalty of receiving Thirty Nine lashes on their bare backs . . . ."[21] Despite the threat of sterner penalties, the ordinance proved ineffectual.

Urban slaves also performed certain civic duties. Negroes worked with their masters or in lieu of them to maintain the town's streets. Free blacks, such as Solomon Cumbo, a mulatto, were required to work so many days a year on the streets or pay a fine, but roadwork was assigned all freemen in the colony. Wilmington actually relieved freemen of this responsibility in 1774 when it employed James Grant "to oversee the Cleansing of the Streets of this Town, & [declared] that he have power to hire six negroes to work thereon, for which he is to be allowed Six Shillings per day for himself & three Shillings for each of the negroes per day. . . ." Other blacks manned the town's fire engines.[22]

White Carolinians never satisfactorily solved the dilemmas endemic to urban slavery. A 1785 act by the legislature resorted to the use of badges for Negroes, bond and free, "to Regulate and Restrain the[ir] Conduct" in Wilmington, Washington, Edenton, and Fayetteville. The statute rehearsed a litany of familiar abuses by the black population: "there are many slaves in the said towns, who contrary to law have houses of their own, or are permitted to reside in the outhouses or kitchens of divers of the inhabitants, or in the houses of the free negroes, mulattoes, persons of mixed blood and others, and work and labour for themselves in several trades and occupations, stipulating to pay their owners such daily, weekly or monthly wages as shall be demanded of them; by reason of which robberies and frauds frequently happen, servants are corrupted, and the poor white inhabitants are deprived of the means of earning their subsistence by labour." According to the new law, only masters could contract and receive the monies earned by slaves who were hired out. Those slaves, moreover, had to wear badges and become subject to the towns' taxes. In order to discriminate between free blacks and slaves, free Negroes had to register with the town commissioners, pay a fee, and wear a "badge of cloth . . . to be fixed on the left shoulder, and to have thereon wrought in legible capital letters the word FREE."[23]

The anomaly afflicting all southern society was thus manifest in this 1785 statute—free Negroes violated the integrity of the institution of slavery, offered alternate models for black behavior, inspired black aspirations for freedom, and undermined the foundations of the South's social and economic system. Even though white Carolinians discouraged manumission and placed high barriers around the slave population, the free black population continued to grow in eighteenth-century North Carolina.

Before the American Revolution there were few free blacks in the South. The only census of blacks in the colonial period was taken in Maryland in 1755 where 1,800 Negro freemen were counted, of whom about 80 percent were mixed bloods; they only represented 4.7 percent of the black population in the state. William Gaston, chief justice of the North Carolina Supreme Court, noted in 1835 "that previous to the Revolution there were scarcely any emancipated Slaves in this State; and that the few free men of color that were here at that time, were chiefly Mulattoes, the children of white women."[24]

Though outlawed in the slave codes of 1715 and 1741, miscegenation and even interracial marriages, if not prevalent, were not uncommon. Most often free blacks were the progeny of white mothers or conscience-stricken white fathers. The Reverend John Blacknall of Edenton was fined £50 in 1725 for joining "together in the holy estate of Matrimony according to the form of the Church of England ... Thomas Spencer a White man and a molatto Woman named Martha paul both of Curratuck precinct contrary to an Act of Assembly ...."[25] According to Josiah Quincy, a Massachusetts revolutionary visiting North Carolina in 1773, the "enjoyment of a negro or mulatto woman is spoken of as quite a common thing: no reluctance, delicacy or shame is made about the matter."[26] During the 1780s a Spanish traveler who was entertained at the Lower Cape Fear plantation of Robert Howe, North Carolina's highest ranking Continental officer during the Revolutionary War, recorded that Howe's "lovely daughter, eighteen years old, has just had two sons by one of the Negro slaves."[27]

Even so, interracial sexual activity usually provoked the censure of the white community. A Jamaican merchant on the road from Charlestown to North Carolina reported: "I found an empty House, the late Tenant of which had been oblig'd by the Church Wardens to decamp on Account of his having kept a Black Woman. Dont suppose Fornication is out of Fashion here more than in other Places, No! the difference only is, that the White Girls monopolize it."[28]

Miscegenation sometimes had salutary effects. A traveler journeying from New Bern to Wilmington in the 1770s was astounded by an eight-mile long causeway through the swamps near the Trent River at a time when North Carolina had notoriously bad roads. He learned that the daughter of the overseer of the road "was delivered of a Mulatto Child." The desperate girl asked a midwife if "it was possible for a Woman to be got with Child when she was asleep without her knowing it, &c: the Overseer of the Road, Believing the Fact to be as it was, & finding it would go hard with his Daughter, compromised the Matter as well as he could, & in Order to have Satisfaction of his Neighbors, altered the Road & made them come & make this Causeway through a Swamp."[29]

Though the taboo on interracial sexual relations was a sensitive issue on which there was widespread agreement throughout the South, colonial regulation of free blacks was often inconsistent and ambiguous in other respects. In North Carolina free blacks served in the militia, just as all other freemen, with no apparent discrimination until the nineteenth century when they could only serve as musicians. A muster roll for the Granville County militia in 1754 listed in Captain John Glover's company: William Chavers, Negro; William Chavers, Jr., mulatto; Gilbert Chavers, mulatto; and Edward Harris, Negro. Captain Osborn Jeffrey's company contained five mulattoes: Thomas Gowen, Michael Gowen, Edward Gowen, Robert Davis, and William Burnel.[30] Maryland, on the other hand, prohibited free blacks from mustering with the militia.

Similarly, free blacks could vote in North Carolina. Though a 1715 law disallowed Negro voting, the king in 1737 repealed the statute because it permitted freemen as well as freeholders to vote. In 1760 the king instructed the royal governor to limit suffrage to freeholders only, that is, those who held in fee simple or for life an estate of fifty acres of land. That measure, however, did not necessarily disqualify free blacks. The North Carolina Constitution of 1776, moreover, made no distinction between races for suffrage. That free blacks voted before their disfranchisement in 1835 is a matter of record. At one time an estimated 300 black electors were registered in Halifax County.[31]

Free blacks, nevertheless, unquestionably suffered various forms of discrimination. The 1723 act which extended taxation on free blacks to their spouses and children over twelve years of age was especially burdensome. No other white women were taxed, and the scarcity of specie made taxes especially oppressive. The law admittedly was designed to discourage intermarriage of the races and to compel free Negroes to wed "those of their own complection. . . ." Petitions to the General Assembly in the 1760s and 1770s contained the signatures of whites principally but also some blacks requesting that the offensive statute of 1723 be repealed. Originating in Northampton, Edgecombe, and Granville counties, the petitions characterized the free Negroes and mulattoes as "persons of Probity and good Demeanor [who] . . . cheerfully contribute towards the discharge of every public Duty," in obvious reference to militia service and roadwork and possibly voting. One petition termed the discriminatory tax as "highly Derogatory of the Rights of Freeborn Subjects."[32]

Clearly some free Negroes enjoyed the respect and confidence of the white community. A Continental officer at Williamsborough in 1782 observed the following amusing scene at a tavern: "The first thing I saw on my Entrance was a Free Malatto and a White man seated on the Hearth foot, to foot, Playing all fours by firelight: a Dollar a Game."[33]

But tensions between free blacks and whites could just as often poison any reservoir of good will between the two races. Free black artisans faced stiff competition from whites and from slaves who were hired out. Disputes over land, jobs, or taxes could cast free blacks in a suspicious light. Reporting on the king's lands in Bladen County in 1773, nervous whites vaguely denounced a group of twenty "free Negars and Mulattus" who had "traitorously assembled together."[34] Ocracoke pilots had more specific charges to make in the same year. They petitioned the assembly to deny licenses to free Negroes and slaves who were piloting vessels up several rivers and back again "to the Great prejudice and Injury of your Petitioners." Obviously the economic competition posed by blacks most concerned the Ocracoke pilots, but they spoke ominously of the "Great Confusion and Irregularity [which] daily Insue from the Insolent and Turbilent disposition and behaviour of such Free negroes and Slaves."[35]

Being a free black in the eighteenth-century South also presented other dangers besides legal disabilities and white fears of economic competition. Freedom could be an ephemeral status. A free Negro named Philip Laneer, "alias Philander," was reenslaved by the North Carolina General Court in 1723 to pay off his former master's debts.[36] John Scott proved more fortunate. Scott's mother "was a free born . . . Mulatto woman," and therefore he too was free. She bound him out as an indentured servant to Robert Yates of Charles County, Maryland, until the age of twenty-one. But in 1766 Yates sold the remaining three years of Scott's indenture to Benjamin Branson, who promptly turned around and sold Scott to a North Carolinian in 1767. In 1770 Scott demanded his freedom, and St. Mary's County Court in Maryland upheld his claim, since it was "a Fact very notorious in the Neighborhood where he lived that he was entitled to Freedom at the Age of twenty one Years."[37]

More heinous, however, was the practice of stealing free Negroes and selling them into slavery. North Carolina did not make it a crime until 1779, but that law only applied to the act of transporting free blacks out of the state. A statute passed in 1801 finally extended the provisions to include violations within the state.[38] The *North Carolina Gazette* reported such a case in 1778. At Broad Creek on the Neuse River two masked men broke into the home of Ann Driggus, a free Negro woman, beat her with clubs, "wounded her terribly and carried away four of her children, three girls and a boy . . . ." The oldest girl escaped.[39] In 1799 the Perquimans County Court ordered three men to post a £1,000 bail bond and to pay £500 in damages to Dolley James, a free black, whom they "with force & arms . . . Assaulted beat & for a long time To wit the Space of Seven Days unlawfully faulsly & without Cause Imprisoned her with Intent to Convey her into foreign parts & Sell & Dispose of her as a Slave. . . ."[40]

In spite of the legal obstacles to manumission and the perils of maintaining their freedom in a slave society, free blacks continued to cope in North Carolina. Samuel Overton's freedom papers issued in Edenton in 1783 stated that the mulatto was "a Free man, and is entituled to all the Rights, Priviledges Immunities of a Citizen of the State of North Carolina." In New Hanover County in 1796 Amelia Green purchased her own freedom for £100 and later that of her daughter Princess, a "certain Negroe or Mollato Girl."[41]

White control of the black population in eighteenth-century North Carolina was pervasive but not suffocating. Slaves and free blacks had to contend with repressive laws and degrading social norms, but the knots in these tethers were not always tight. Black assertiveness carved out areas of freedom, notably in the towns, which white Carolinians never could completely eradicate. If many slaves were content to live their lives safely within the constraints defined by the white community, many others proved less docile and more audacious in their challenge to the social order. They were the ones who most profoundly stirred white fears of servile insurrection.

CHAPTER III

Rebels, Runaways, Religionists

The reactions of newly enslaved Africans and American-born blacks to bondage defy simple categorizations such as docility or violent resistance. Within each slave could exist the seeds of both, and an individual's response to slavery at any point in time must be plotted along a continuum between the two extremes. Rebelliousness could be overt or disguised, violent or peaceable, explicit in a gesture and tone of voice or implicit in a broken tool and feigned illness. Whatever form resistance to slavery took, it inevitably proved unsettling to the white community, for as patterns of white domination hardened blacks continually tested the outer limits of their circumscribed lives. Running away, of course, represented the most visible sign of slave unrest, but religion—despite the efforts of some slaveholders either to discourage or control it—burst the spiritual bonds of southern society and permitted slaves to shape their own version of Christianity and articulate their innermost yearnings for freedom. In so doing, black religion became a powerful counterweight to the everyday indignities and frustrations of slavery.

Black criminality is hard to define within the context of a slave society since legal shackles and social norms restricted all sorts of human behavior. But there were in fact a few ornery Negroes who made their livings through crime. When the notorious pirate Edward Teach, more popularly known as Blackbeard, was slain in North Carolina waters and his crew captured in 1718, among the captives were five Negro pirates. The Virginia Council, acting with Governor Alexander Spotswood, who had authorized the expedition against Blackbeard, found the five blacks guilty of piracy along with the rest of the crew.[1] North Carolina's Governor Gabriel Johnston complained to the Board of Trade in London in 1749 that for two years the colony's coast had suffered repeated raids from Spanish-held St. Augustine in Florida by sloops "full of armed men, mostly Mulattoes & Negroes" who landed at Ocracoke, Bear Inlet, and Cape Fear. According to the royal governor, they burned ships, killed several people, slaughtered cattle and hogs, and "carried off some Negroes."[2]

Sea-going brigands were something of a rarity, however, for Carolina slaveholders only had to look to their homes and farms to find black rebelliousness. The trials of Mrs. Jean Blair, a member of the politically and socially prestigious Johnston family, reveal much about the inner-workings of a biracial family unit and the labor patterns of independent-minded slaves. Slaves' malingering or insolence toward white directives could define the limits of their work, the hours they labored, and even when and how they performed their duties. The constant challenge to the system and testing of boundaries inexorably eroded white authority and expanded black autonomy.

Mrs. Blair, an able and intelligent woman, found handling a household of slaves no simple chore. Her difficulties were exacerbated by the war ravaging North Carolina in 1781. "I hardly ever knew the trouble of house keeping before," she wrote, "a large family and continual confusion and not any thing to eat but salt meat and hoe cake and no conveniences to dress them." When the family was struck by illness, she discovered: "Aggy is better but thinks it a great hardship that she should be obliged to work when she is so weak and low tho' she is well enough to go abroad." Getting the slaves to stay in Windsor, moreover, when the family home and connections were in Edenton proved exasperating at best. "Andrew and Simon went down [to Edenton] on friday," she explained to Revolutionary leader James Iredell, "which obliged me to let my Brothers Negroe go home too as he had nobody to assist him. He returned yesterday and so did Simon. Andrew promised to return last night or this morning but is not yet come and Peter says he does not think he will be here till next week. I think he behaves very ill. He ought either to have staid till he was done or made more haste up."[3] Calculated dilatoriness or carelessness became artfully cultivated traits to disguise patterns of resistance to slavery.

There was nothing subtle or guileful, however, about Sarah's insolent attitude at being brought from Edenton to Windsor to assist with the new household. As a house slave, Sarah doubtless was accustomed to certain amenities and working conditions most slaves could only dream about. Still her displeasure could not be disguised. Mrs. Blair grumbled: "She thinks herself so ill used to be brought into [Such a mess] before I had prepared a tight house for her with a lock to it and thinks I had more [slaves] before than I had work for. . . . but if she gives herself many more airs she shall never see Edenton again. Very little more will provoke me to sell her. Andrew behaves very well and so does old Simon but Peter seems unwilling to be here and thinks there are enough without him. I daresay it is Sarah that makes him so dis[s]atisfied. She never came near me till after repeated messages yesterday to her to come and Iron a few clothes. . . . She made shift to creep here just in the evening and then was very impudent. If she does not behave much better I will hire her here. . . ."[4] Mrs. Blair's threats probably had little effect, for clearly the slaves set the pace of and ran the household as much as she did.

Perhaps the most prevalent form of resistance to slavery was theft. Though slaveholders continually deplored their bondsmen's thievery, many came to expect it and to a certain degree to tolerate it. As shown earlier, numerous statutes and town ordinances attempted to curb the illicit black market which sprang up among blacks and between whites and slaves. Thefts by slaves appeared in the public records of North Carolina as early as the seventeenth century. The slave Mingo was accused of "Running away from the house of Daniel Akehurst, Esqr. and Carrying away severall goods belonging to him" in 1685. Another court document reported in 1698 that three slaves—two Negroes and an Indian—in the absence of their master "rob[b]ed the house and Caryed away Severall Goods and a trunk with wearing Cloathes. . . ."[5] But as the status of slaves deteriorated during the eighteenth century and their opportunities became more limited, they increasingly resorted to the hazardous practice of taking what they needed, or were deprived of, and using or trading it to suit their own purposes.

A number of blacks simply became highwaymen. At a trial in Wilmington in 1768, a Negro named Quamino was charged with robbing a number of persons. Cornelius Harnett, the Revolutionary leader, presided at the trial. Quamino was found guilty and sentenced "to be hang'd by the Neck until he is dead . . . and his head to be affixed up upon the Point near Wilmington."[6] A sailor traveling overland from Norfolk to Edenton had the misfortune to be "robbed on the road of 49$ and some cloathes by a negro (who is supposed to be a negro named Peter formerly the Proper[t]y of Jet Benton in Gates) about half way between here & Norfolk."[7]

Stealing by slaves is best illustrated by the frequent disappearance of livestock. Colonial newspapers in Virginia, North Carolina, and South Carolina are replete with notices of horses or cattle "strayed or stolen." Working on a daily basis with livestock, slaves had easy access to these valuable animals. The slave code eventually barred bondsmen from keeping horses, cattle, or hogs. But that did not prevent blacks from rustling or "appropriating" meat for their tables. Negro Sam was found guilty of feloniously "presenting a gun at Capt. Cornelius Ryan and for Breaking open David Ryan's Smoke House and taking a parcel of meat. . . ." He was hanged.[8] In 1748 a slave named Cato was tried for killing a hog as he was grinding at a mill; he claimed that he did not know the hog was his mistress's. Cato, however, escaped execution. The court ruled that "the Sheriff take the said Negro Cato to the Publick whiping Post & there to nail his Ears to the said Post & . . . [to] Cut [them] off then to be whipped at the said post with 40 Lashes well laid on. . . ."[9]

Theft, verbal insolence, and malingering were types of resistance that most slaves probably engaged in at one time or another in their lives. But more lethal kinds of resistance also threatened the white community. One form—of indisputably African origin—was poisoning. Conjurers or obeah-men held great influence within the slave community. In West Africa obeah-men were skilled practitioners in the use of roots and herbs for medicinal purposes and for combating various poisons. Slaves listed with the name "Doctor" had doubtless earned their honors. A Virginia Negro was given his freedom and a lifetime pension by

THE VOODOO DANCE.

The obeah-man wielded great influence in the slave community. Casting spells and mixing potions, the conjurer was considered the healer of the sick and avenger of the wronged. Kemble sketch from the *Century Magazine*, XXXI (1885-1886), 816.

37

the colonial government for discovering a treatment for certain distempers. Among blacks the obeah-man was known as the healer of the sick, interpreter of the unknown, comforter of the sad, and avenging agent of the wronged with his supernatural powers.[10]

Accorded such reputations for power by other blacks, obeah-men wielded enormous influence. At the 1779 trial of Bristoe, a Johnston County slave, the role of the obeah-man in the slave community was evident. For the slave Jacob, Bristoe prepared a concoction "to make his master sell him." To a slave woman he gave a potion of milk to prevent her having children. For still another slave Bristoe poured brandy in a hole in the ground and gave the supplicant a root to chew "to make his master Buy his wife...." Obviously fearing Bristoe's powers but not quite knowing how to deal with him, the court ordered that he be given thirty lashes.[11]

That Carolina blacks used their knowledge of herbal medicines and poisons to rebel against white dominance is clear. In 1780 the Johnston County slave court tried Jenny for poisoning her master Needham Bryan. She denied the charges, but two whites and four Negroes gave evidence against her. The court found her guilty of murder and sentenced her "to be bur[n]t to Death by a Stake."[12]

The uses of herbs and potions as resistance had other applications besides murder. The curious case of Will, a Dobbs County slave, is revealing. In 1769 Will went to the home of Sarah Wiggens, the wife of Gursham Wiggens, and offered her a drink of rum. At first she refused, according to her own testimony, but later relented. The rum, she said, made her "strangely sick," so Will produced a bottle containing herbs to help cure her illness. Instead the potion intoxicated her "and took away her Senses." Thereafter Will returned "at different times" with "some Liquid thing to drink which always deprived her of her Senses, and by that means had Carnal knowledge of her Body...." Subsequently she had a child by Will, but he threatened to poison any person who "would or did talk about it...." She feared Will might poison her. He "told her that if ever she turned against him he would do something to her that would kill or otherwise destroy her—and that the said Will by behaving in The Manner above mentioned had Carnal knowledge of her divers times and was the father of her last Child...." Will's knowledge of herbs and roots was such that he boasted "he could lye with the best of the Women" in the county if he wished.[13] Sarah Wiggens might have been trying to cover up an interracial dalliance or explain the birth of her mulatto child, but the probability that Will was a conjurer must surely have had its effect on the white community, not a few of whom probably wondered what his aphrodisiac contained.

Individual acts of aggression or violence toward slaveholders were almost always suicidal. No matter the provocation, Carolina blacks had to develop strict internal constraints against showing strong emotions like anger. A hostile look or gesture by a slave could bring a terrible retribution. Two white men swore before the Perquimans County Court in 1706 that they were "in bodily fear of a negro calld Dick. . . ." The court ruled that Dick be taken into custody until his master "shall become bound with good & Sufficient Security for the Sᵈ Negroes good abearance. . . ."[14] The Committee of Claims in the General Assembly, as already noted, reviewed scores of petitions for compensation of executed slaves, many of whom were convicted of murder. In Halifax County in 1785, the slave Peter was found guilty of murdering John Miller and Sarah Gold. He was hanged, his head cut off and placed on a pole, and his body burned.[15] Five of Henry Ormond's slaves conspired to kill the Beaufort County planter. First they attempted to strangle him as he slept but failed. According to one account, he begged "earnestly" for his life but was told that he "must die." His "house wench, told him it was in vain, that as he had no mercy on them, he could expect none himself." They thereupon suffocated him between two feather beds. "The slaves have been tried, two wenches executed, and one burnt at a stake, one made his escape, and is not yet taken, the other who made the confession, is saved."[16]

Violence among slaves—black against black—was not unknown. Quarrels over lovers or personal grudges accounted for many instances of murder or manslaughter, but the sources are silent as to precise details. In 1786 the slave Sam was hanged by Halifax County authorities for "poisoning a Negroe Woman Named Sue . . . ."[17] Similarly, Granville County whites speculated that the slave Jack, found "barbarously and willfully" murdered, had been slain by a runaway named Swift.[18] The murder may have been an example of old African tribal feuds which continued to fester in the colonial South, or perhaps Jack threatened to reveal Swift's whereabouts. Some Negroes, whom white Carolinians deemed the most loyal, clearly had internalized the values of their masters. William Bryan of Craven County received £50 from the General Assembly in 1783 "for a negro man slave killed in suppressing of Rebel Slaves. . . ."[19] In New Hanover County in

1760, a "Negro man named Jack—belonging to Mr. John Dalrumple was shot by a Negro man named Paris belonging to Mr. Dalrumple aforesaid for stealing sundry things out of his said Masters House as the sd. Negro Paris had positive Orders from his Mistress to shott any Negroes whome he could apprehend breaking open the House. . . ."[20]

Slave rebelliousness in any form disquieted white Carolinians, but no single act of self-assertion by blacks alarmed them more than running away. Not only was running away costly in terms of time and money lost, but it also imperiled the security of the white community. Runaways plagued Carolina planters almost as soon as Africans began to be imported into the colony. As early as the 1680s planters bewailed the Negroes running off to St. Augustine, Florida. In 1698 the North Carolina General Court reported the capture of "four sturdy runaway slaves" from Virginia who had killed three hogs "and appeared in armes and made resistance. . . ." Thomas Pollock, one of the largest land-holders in the colony, could not attend the Court of Chancery near the turn of the eighteenth century because two of his slaves had "newly runaway and I believe are Joyned to a moletto belonging to Captain Goodine of Virginy. . . ." Pollock explained the danger posed by runaways: "I must use my indeavors to have them catched iff possible least they should gather to a greater head and doe mischiefe on this shore which I have greatt reasons to suspect." The threat of servile insurrection menaced his family's and community's safety, for if he did not apprehend the absentees "more of my Negroes might runaway and indanger" the colony.[21]

North Carolina during the eighteenth century had a reputation as a haven for slave fugitives. Since Virginians were among the numerous settlers swelling the colony's population at mid-century, it was inevitable that slave families were broken up thereby compelling slaves left behind to run south to reunite families. The colony also attracted an exceptionally skilled group of slaves who found North Carolina less oppressive than Virginia. Of the recorded instances of slaves fleeing Virginia before 1775, the number headed for North Carolina far exceeded the number trying for other destinations. From the seventeenth century on, Virginians complained about runaways to North Carolina. John Tayloe's Billy, aged thirty, fled to North Carolina in 1768 where he "travelled without much interruption" with a pass, in all likelihood

40

forged. Billy's skill as a violinist may have contributed to his affability, but his craftsmanship as a ship's carpenter doubtless aided his freedom. Likewise William Trebell's Bob ran away from a plantation near Williamsburg in 1767 and was captured in Hertford County, North Carolina. There he had lived with a small farmer named Van Pelt on the Chinkopin River. Having passed as a freeman, Bob could read and write, do carpentry, and perform as a "very good sailor." Moreover, he had married in North Carolina.[22]

The following advertisement in the *Virginia Gazette* in 1767 provides a vivid depiction of a fugitive slave headed for North Carolina:

> Run away about the 15th of December last, a small yellow Negro wench named Hannah, about 35 years of age; had on when she went away a green plains petticoat, and sundry other clothes, but what sort I do not know, as she stole many from the other Negroes. She has remarkable long hair, or wool, is much scarified under the throat from one ear to the other, and has many scars on her back, occasioned by whipping. She pretends much to the religion the Negroes of late have practised, and may probably endeavor to pass for a free woman. . . . She is supposed to have made for Carolina.[23]

North Carolinians did not seem to hold too many scruples when it came to using somebody else's slave. Runaways with much-needed skills quickly melted into the colony's black population. With its vast forests and swamps, sparsely populated regions, and numerous rivers and creeks flowing southeast, North Carolina absorbed many runaways from Virginia. The Roanoke and Chowan rivers with their interconnections with Virginia waterways made such eastern counties as Bute and Halifax likely havens for runaways. Lacking large tidewater slaveholders, North Carolina's middling society of nonslaveholding yeomen attracted slave fugitives. Black carters, carpenters, sawyers, millwrights, and other artisans found willing accomplices in North Carolina where the economy, based in large part on forest products, could readily employ them.[24]

Not all runaways, of course, managed to pass as free or accepted reenslavement by North Carolina masters. Fugitives from Virginia and North Carolina quickly made the Great Dismal Swamp, stretching nearly from Edenton to Norfolk, a sanctuary for runaways. With its trackless waters and dense vegetation, the swamp was an ideal hideout. One observer noted that in the swamps the runaways were "perfectly safe, and with the greatest facility elude the most diligent search of their pursuers." Some blacks had lived there "for twelve, twenty, or thirty years and upwards, subsisting themselves . . . upon corn, hogs, and fowls. . . ." The runaways cleared small fields for habitation which were not subject to flooding, but "perfectly impenetrable to any of the inhabitants of the country around. . . ."[25] Another traveler reported in 1777 that the Dismal Swamp "was infested by concealed royalists, and runaway negroes, who could not be approached with safety. They often attacked travellers, and had recently murdered a Mr. Williams." One man was supposedly confronted by "fourteen naked negroes, armed with poles, [who] presented themselves in the attitude of hostility, across the road." He nevertheless managed to escape.[26]

The Dismal Swamp was not the only region in the colony harassed by bands of runaways. The New Hanover County Court in 1767 reported that "upwards of Twenty run away Slaves in abody Arm'd" were at large and ordered "that the Sheriff do immediately raise the power of the County not to be less than Thirty Men well Arm'd, to go in pursuit of the said run away Slaves and that the said Sheriff be impowered to Shoot Kill & destroy all such of the said run away Slaves as shall not Surrender themselves."[27]

Historians have only recently begun to analyze quantifiable data on runaway slaves in the colonial South. As indicated earlier, Gerald W. Mullin has found a disproportionate number of black artisans who ran away in Virginia and frequently headed for North Carolina. Investigating similar data for South Carolina, Peter Wood argues that runaways came from every level of the slave community, though a skilled craftsman usually stood the best chance of obtaining his freedom permanently. The vast majority of fugitives were simply field hands. Men tended to run off more frequently than women, but women were more likely to visit other slaves and then return of their own accord. Certainly the number of runaways advertised in colonial newspapers represented only a small percentage of the actual number of absentees, for advertising was generally only as a last resort and usually confined to those slaveholders who could afford the cost and the reward. Many slaves were caught before a notice became necessary; others returned on their own initiative.[28]

The reasons why a slave fled were diverse and complex. Some blacks manifestly desired their freedom no matter what the cost. If unable to join other maroons in a swamp, a fugitive's best hope might lie to the south in the sparsely settled wilderness of Florida where the Spanish could offer protection from the Anglo-Americans. The North in colonial America did not represent the lodestar of freedom which it would become in later decades. Others sought to reunite families or simply could no longer tolerate the cruel treatment of a brutal master. Some merely sulked in the woods for a few days after a conflict with the master and then returned. Running away was also an effective means of bargaining with the master over some cause of complaint; it made a master more willing to make an adjustment desired by the slave.

While the data for runaways in North Carolina is rather sketchy because of the sporadic publication of newspapers and the relative dearth of other sources when compared with South Carolina or Virginia, runaway patterns generally fell along three lines. First, slaves who had been hired out or recently sold to a new master had a great propensity for flight. Such transitions and dislocations fostered strong anxieties among blacks. Often these blacks did not seek permanent freedom but rather the opportunity to return to families and familiar surroundings, or kinder masters. The slave Dick, hired out by the Blount family, was determined to run away because "of very hard usage." Dick warned that he would continue to flee "if he ever gets an opportunity."[29] Similarly, Micaj Thomas told Thomas Blount that the "negro wench I purchased of you is Run away and I have reason to beleave that She is gon back to washington.... I ... expect She will indeavour to git back to where She was Raised, but am convinced that She will call for her Husband. . . ."[30] John Wallace, however, evidently faced a more serious challenge. He wrote John Gray Blount: "4 of the Negroes I hiered from Cove Sound Stold our Boat on Saturday night and Ran away. . . ." Those slaves doubtless meant to escape to freedom. Only one had been recaptured with the boat; the others remained at large.[31]

A second grouping of runaways included recently imported Africans who, shocked and bewildered by their debarkation and sale, defected. They were the least acculturated slaves, carrying the marks and scars of African rituals, bearing African names, and speaking little or no English. A runaway from Wilmington was described as "a new Negro Fellow, by name Quamino ... [who] has a Scar above his right Eye, his Teeth are filed, and [he] is marked with his Country Marks; had on when he went away, a Collar about his Neck with two prongs, marked G.P., and an iron on each Leg."[32] A Negro named Will captured in Craven

County had "a mark in his forehead imitating a diamond, a circle round each eye (supposed to be his country mark) but two toes on his right foot. . . ."[33] A group of "Five newly imported Slaves"—four men and a woman—ran off from New Bern though they were "incapable of uttering a Word of *English*."[34] One African—"a Congoer"—boldly demanded that his master sell him and his wife and two children. The slaveholder was unwilling but feared that the African "will not stay here."[35] The sheriff of Craven County offered this glimpse of the runaways sequestered in the New Bern jail in 1767:

> Two New Negro Men, the one named Joe, about 45 years of age, . . . much wrinkled in the face, and speaks bad English. The other is a young fellow, . . . speaks better English than Joe, who he says is his father, has a large scar on the fleshy part of his left arm. . . . They have nothing with them but an old Negro cloth jacket, and an old blue sailors jacket without sleeves. Also . . . a Negro named Jack, about 23 years of age, . . . of a thin visage, blear eyed, . . . has six rings of his country marks around his neck, his ears full of holes. . . .[36]

Desperate and confused, African newcomers swelled the numbers of runaways who kept Carolina slaveholders in a state of agitation.

Finally the third type of slave likely to strike for freedom, as in Virginia, was the skilled artisan. Combining their intelligence with talents, these resourceful slaves could pass as free Negroes or outwit their white pursuers. One runaway, appropriately named Smart, was described as "very black, . . . well made, and very likely, [who] speaks broken English, but [is] very artful and insinuating. He is supposed to be lurking about *Slocomb's* Creek, with a Fellow belonging to Mr. *Almond*, and a Gang of Runaways belonging to the late Mr. Clear's Estate."[37] Abraham, a runaway mulatto, showed verve, imagination, and style in his flight. Characterized as "very likely and well made," he was a "tolerable good house carpenter and shoemaker." Abraham took with him plenty of clothes and a considerable sum of money, and he "appear[ed] well dressed." Moreover, he had escaped with another mulatto named Lewis, and both were on horseback. The advertisement suggested that they would probably change their names "and endeavour to pass as freemen." They were believed to be headed for South Carolina to catch a vessel to the West Indies since Abraham had relatives in St. Eustatia.[38]

Running away carried immense risks. Mutilation, whipping, irons and chains, or even death might befall a fleet-footed slave.

John Brickell, noting the recalcitrance of African newcomers, observed in 1737: "There are great numbers of them [Negroes] born here, which prove more industrious, honest, and better Slaves than any brought from *Guinea*; this is particularly owing to their Education amongst the *Christians*, which very much polishes and refines them from their barbarous and stubborn Natures that they are most commonly endued with." Kemble sketch from the *Century Magazine*, XXXI (1885-1886), 813.

Moreover, capture at the hands of white men proved preferable to ensnarement by Indians. Relations between blacks and Indians remained ambiguous throughout the colonial period. Negroes escaping westward risked betrayal, captivity, and death. Some blacks, to be sure, were absorbed into the Indian culture, but many more appear to have been pawns caught in the delicate frontier diplomacy of native Americans and European colonists. One of the principal demands of white negotiators all through the colonial and Revolutionary period continued to be the return of runaways by the Indians.

John Brickell explained the additional dangers faced by black absentees: "The *Negroes* sometimes make use of ... Advantages in the Woods, where they will stay for Months together before they can be found out by their Masters, or any other Person; and great Numbers of them would act after the same manner (which would be detrimental to the Planters) were they not so much afraid of the *Indians*, who have such a natural aversion to the *Blacks*, that they commonly shoot them when ever they find them in the Woods or solitary parts of the Country." Indians were often employed to track down runaways, and, according to Brickell, they "commonly kill many of them [Negroes] whenever they are sent in pursuit...." The Indians allegedly took "Pleasure in putting them to the most exquisite Torments, when ever they find them thus in the Woods...."[39] At Christmas time in 1765 at the height of the Stamp Act crisis, slave unrest intensified as the political situation became increasingly unstable, particularly in Charlestown. Many South Carolina Negroes fled to the swamps, generating white fears of "some dangerous Conspiracy and Insurrection." The South Carolina governor invited the Catawba Indians of North Carolina "to come down and hunt the Negroes. . . . The Indians immediately came and partly by the Terror of their name their Diligence and singular sagacity in pursuing Enemies thro such Thickets soon dispersed the runaway Negroes, apprehended several and the most of the rest of them chose to surrender themselves to their Masters and return to their Duty rather than expose themselves to the attack of an Enemy so dreaded. . . ."[40] By the middle of the eighteenth century Cherokees, Creeks, and Catawbas had built such reputations for capturing runaways that a certain class of braves held the distinctive title "slave catcher."[41]

Despite the prevalence of runaways, then, the chances of obtaining permanent freedom remained minimal and the risks of capture or worse high. Still some blacks simply refused to accept reenslavement. The New Hanover County Court in 1766 recorded such a poignant instance: "A Negro fellow named London, who belonged to the Hon. Lewis Henry DeRosset, Esq. and ran away and was outlawed, upon being taken up jumped into the river and drowned himself. . . ."[42]

Resistance to slavery had its spiritual as well as secular side. If religion could not free the Afro-American of his or her bonds, it could nourish the spirit and provide an outlet for Negro yearnings for freedom. Moreover, despite initial misgivings on the part of Carolina slaveholders about converting Africans, Christianity made rapid gains in the slave community throughout the eighteenth century. Riding the waves of religious fervor released by the First Great Awakening of the 1730s and 1740s and the Second Great Awakening of 1800 to 1805, evangelical Protestantism washed over the white and black communities like a flood. Evangelical Protestantism did more than supplant the Church of England and contribute to the Anglicans' disestablishment in 1776; it also challenged the social order in insidious ways which loosened traditional constraints over blacks, a trend not fully reversed until the second decade of the nineteenth century.

Anglican missionaries early in the colonial period attempted to convert the African bondsmen, but they faced an uphill struggle.

To begin with, the Anglican church never attained great strength in North Carolina and had no certain establishment until the Vestry Act of 1765. That statute was quickly overturned by the new state Constitution of 1776 which disestablished the Church of England. More problematic were the slaveholders themselves who opposed religious instruction or baptism for Negroes despite guarantees in the Fundamental Constitutions that the slave status of a black convert was in no way altered. James Adams, an Anglican cleric, noted in 1709 that planters would not permit the baptism of their slaves, "having a false notion that a Christian slave is by law free." Another Anglican minister declared in 1719 that Negroes in North Carolina were "sensible and civil and . . . inclined to Christianity and . . . would be converted, baptized, and saved, if their masters were not so wicked as they are, and did not oppose their conversion, baptism, and salvation, so much as they do."[43] In 1730 the crown finally instructed royal Governor George Burrington "to find out the best means to facilitate & encourage the conversion of Negroes and Indians to the Christian religion."[44]

Carolina slaveholders recognized that certain Christian tenets were subversive, particularly the notion of brotherhood among all men. Consequently, no white minister could give a full exegesis of the gospel without risking the wrath of the planters. Pious slaveholders insisted that religion emphasize obedience by slaves. "Servants obey your masters" provided the theme for countless sermons in the slaveholding South.[45] Nevertheless by the 1740s slave baptisms had increased significantly in North Carolina. Anglican clergymen, writing the secretary of the Society for the Propagation of the Gospel (S.P.G.), reported numerous baptisms and conversions among whites and blacks. Charles Cupples informed the S.P.G. in 1768 that in Bute County he had "baptized 382 children, 51 of which were negro children [;] the engagements for some were made by their Masters and Mistresses, and others had God fathers and God mothers of their own color as having been formerly baptized. . . ."[46] Another missionary in Northampton County reported in 1772 that he had performed baptisms for "46 Black infants, [and] 55 Black Adults, who seem to be very desirous of instruction in their duty."[47]

Anglican clerics also took the lead in trying to educate blacks and Indians. A society called Dr. Bray's Associates established several schools in North Carolina shortly before the Revolution, but its effectiveness was handicapped by the "mean low Prejudices of the People." Whites objected to their children attending school with slaves, and slaveholders criticized the loss of time when blacks left their chores. As one Anglican missionary put it, the slaveholders "would rather their Slaves wou'd remain Ignorant as brutes."[48] The Reverend James Reed of New Bern perhaps best summarized the frustrations of Anglican clergymen when he wrote: "the greatest part of the negroes in the whole country, may to [o] justly be accounted heathens [;] 'tis impossible for ministers in such extensive counties, to instruct them in the principles of the Christian religion & their masters will not take the least pains to do it themselves. I baptize all those whose masters become sureties for them, but never baptize any negro infants or Children upon any other terms."[49]

The process by which Afro-Americans embraced Christianity and shaped it in light of African preconceptions to their particular needs will probably never be fully understood. Vestiges of Islamic religion, for instance, persisted well into the nineteenth century.[50] But for those blacks who became Christians, African folkways sometimes merged with conventional religious beliefs. Such syncretisms were most evident in the frenzied praise meetings, punctuated with perpetual motion and constant singing. An entire congregation kept time with the music by swaying back and forth or patting the hand or foot. The Negro quarters rang with "jubilant shouts."[51]

Dr. Edward Warren left a remarkable account of his visits to Somerset Place—Josiah Collins's plantation on the shore of Lake Scuppernong in eastern North Carolina—which sheds light on the African carry-overs suffusing the slaves' religion. Among the bondsmen at Somerset Place, Dr. Warren reported, were a number of old "Guinea negroes" who had been imported from Africa well before the turn of the nineteenth century. Though Christians, these Africans retained many of the ideas and traditions of their native land. According to Dr. Warren, "they still had faith in evil genii, charms, philters, metempsychosis, etc., and they habitually indulged in an infinitude of cabalistic rites and ceremonies, in which the gizzards of chickens, the livers of dogs, the heads of snakes and the tails of lizards played a mysterious but very conspicuous part."

The one custom that Dr. Warren recalled with particular clarity was called "John Koonering." At Christmas a slave leader—perhaps the obeah-man—dressed in a costume of rags, animal skins, horns, and bells, while a second slave, wearing no disguise but arrayed in his best clothes, carried a small bowl or tin cup and accompanied the "rag man." Others, playing musical instruments or "gumba boxes," followed the leading two characters. They approached the front door of the master's house and commenced performing energetic songs and dances. As a reward or gift, the master was expected to jingle the tin cup with coins. Dr. Warren maintained that during his residence in Egypt he witnessed "a performance absolutely identical with that which I had seen in Carolina" when Egyptian blacks celebrated "Byram—the principal feast of the Koran."[52]

Sustaining such African and Muslim practices suggests the ways in which newcomers came to understand or relate to the religion of their masters. But Christianity could not always provide the emotional release and dissipation of anxieties that African folkways did, sometimes with tragic results. About the same time that Dr. Warren observed the "John Koonering" celebration, other Africans nearby were laboring to drain the swamps, build canals, and create arable land for cultivation. Many blacks died from the hardships. At night the Africans would sing mournful native songs. Overwrought with grief, some bundled up their personal effects and, marching eastward toward Africa, plunged into the waters of Lake Phelps, drowning themselves. These repeated suicides forced slaveholders to stop the evening sings.[53]

Other denominations besides the Anglicans took up the task of converting blacks to Christianity. Presbyterians and Quakers, as early as 1771, were teaching slaves and free blacks to read and write. The Quakers, whose antislavery activities will be discussed in subsequent chapters, had very few black members, however. John Chavis, a Revolutionary War veteran and Presbyterian minister, became the foremost free Negro in antebellum North Carolina and the teacher of countless black and white students, among them Senator Willie P. Mangum. The early Moravians owned a few slaves, several of whom became communicants and worshiped regularly as Brothers. However, the elders were quick to point out in 1776 that that did not make a Negro "free and equal of his master." Toward the end of the eighteenth century race distinctions began to surface in the Moravian church. In 1792 the Brethren were admonished that "we must not be ashamed of those Negroes who belong to our community, and . . . let them sit all by themselves in the congregation worship and even during Holy Communion. They are our Brothers and Sisters and different treatment of them will be a disgrace for the community." Nevertheless, by the 1820s a separate Negro church had been formed.[54]

No denominations, however, proved as popular with blacks or succeeded in proselytizing slaves like the Methodists and Baptists. Evangelical Protestantism, with its emphasis on guilt, suffering, and ecstatic release, doubtless appealed to the slaves. The Awakenings of the eighteenth and nineteenth centuries were great social and religious happenings in which people prayed, sang, shouted, and poured out pent-up emotions together. Indeed, one wonders how much the Africans' practice of Christianity influenced the animated revivalism and emphasis on an emotional conversion experience so characteristic of evangelical Protestantism. Moreover, Methodist and Baptist services were conducted in a democratic atmosphere. Members called each other brothers and sisters, stressed fellowship, and conducted affairs on a footing of equality in stark contrast to the rank and deference of the Anglican church. Finally, the Methodists openly espoused abolitionism in their fledgling years. The result of this popular movement of evangelical religion was a serious challenge to the social and religious structure of the colonial South, the implications of which would be felt for decades to come.[55]

The fastest growing religion in antebellum America was Methodism. John Wesley, its founder, never really considered his movement a separate entity apart from the Anglican church. But the activities of his followers rapidly molded a distinct identity for Methodism. Wesley denounced slavery as an evil institution, but it remained to Francis Asbury and Thomas Coke, who established the religion in America, to spread the gospel and stamp out human bondage. Itinerant Methodist preachers were instructed to preach to Negroes as well as to whites on a basis of religious equality. Between 1782 and 1790 the number of Methodists in North Carolina grew to over 8,000 whites and nearly 1,800 blacks. In 1785 Thomas Coke tried to force North Carolina Methodists to make abolition an article of faith. In other words, to become a member one had to free his or her slaves. That policy had been adopted in 1784 by the Christmas Conference in Baltimore. Coke even tried to block the renewal of Methodist clergymen who owned slaves, but he failed.

In the period before the War of 1812 Negroes—slave and free—accounted for about one-third of the Methodists in North Carolina. By the first decade of the nineteenth century separate African churches had been established in Wilmington, New Bern, Fayetteville, and Edenton, and in 1805 Francis Asbury preached to a number of these black congregations. Henry Evans, a free black shoemaker, is credited with starting the Methodist church in Fayetteville in the 1790s. At first only Negroes attended Evans's services, but eventually whites took over the church and became affiliated with other Methodist societies.

Despite success in spreading their religion, Methodists failed to further the cause of abolition. Near New Bern in 1796 Asbury chided the "conduct of some Methodists, that hire out slaves at public places to the highest bidder, to cut skin, and starve them; I think such members ought to be dealt with." Six years later he castigated slaveholders who would not allow their slaves to hear Methodists or attend a service. After preaching at a church on the New River, he declared: "It was not agreeable to me to see nearly a hundred slaves standing outside and peeping in at the door, whilst the house was half empty: they were not worthy to come in because they were black!" Methodist preachers who gave anti-slavery sermons, however, risked violence as in the case of a Charlestown cleric who was dragged to the town pump and nearly drowned. By 1816 some 42,500 Negroes and 172,000 whites belonged to the Methodist church, but the assault on social institutions had given way to the saving of souls.[56]

If the Methodists' proclivities toward abolitionism disconcerted Carolina whites, then the Baptists' fellowship with slaves seemed even more perfidious. The Baptists permitted slaves to participate fully in worship, a liberty which inexorably unfettered black souls and minds. John Barnett, the Anglican clergyman in Brunswick Town, was clearly befuddled and dumbfounded by this religious equality. "New light baptists," he wrote in 1766, "are very numerous in the southern parts of this parish—The most illiterate among them are their Teachers[;] even Negroes speak in their Meetings."[57] Notices for runaways occasionally identified the fugitives as slave preachers. During the Revolutionary War the *Virginia Gazette* reported an absentee named Will or William Hunt, a skilled blacksmith and shoemaker. "He pretends also to know something of religious matters, and misses no opportunity of holding forth on that subject." The runaway Nat, the newspaper stated, "pretends to be very religious, and is a *Baptist* teacher."[58]

The Baptists attempted to impose order on a disorderly society with slavery at its foundation. That meant inculcating slaves with strict Calvinistic values. Through the eighteenth century blacks and whites worshiped together, and the church's harsh and uncompromising discipline applied to both races. Negroes were accepted into membership the same as whites: the novitiate related a religious experience and, if the congregation were favorably impressed, then accepted into fellowship and baptized. Negroes thus became eligible to participate in Holy Communion and contribute financially to the church's support. When black members moved, they received letters of dismissal from the congregation so as to be placed in another Baptist church.[59]

Testimonies, baptism, and disciplining of whites and blacks took place in common. Any person joining a Baptist church subscribed to its covenant and agreed to abide by rules of decorum. The Sandy Creek Baptist association in present-day Franklin County ruled in 1773 that "Negro Cezar be suspended for Atemting to Preach with oute Leave." In 1792 a slave ironically named Hester and the bondsman Isam were "excommunicated for living in the sin of Adultery."[60]

Baptists seemed especially sensitive to the plight of slave families and therefore proscribed adultery among blacks as vigorously as that among whites. To stabilize slave marriages one Baptist church ruled in 1778 that "the marriage of servants . . . before God" was legitimate despite legal prohibitions. Any member who broke the marriage of slaves could be expelled from fellowship. Masters, moreover, were instructed to permit slaves to attend worship.[61] Another Baptist congregation insisted the slaveholders had a "moral obligation" to keep slave families together, even if it meant "some inconvenience" for the masters. Slave marriages, ordered one Baptist association, would be recognized under these conditions: "no member of color, belonging to this church, shall cohabit with any person as a wife or husband until they have, in the presence of at least two other members of this church, made mutual vows of constancy until death or removal."[62]

Most striking about eighteenth-century Baptists were the black preachers who sermonized mixed congregations. Whereas Anglicans and Presbyterians in particular insisted on a certain level of erudition among their ministers, democratically inclined Baptists were willing to accept preachers moved simply by religious zeal. A "poor African" perhaps stated the Baptist position best: "I perceive . . . that there are many *learned* fools."[63] In the 1780s a predominantly white congregation in Gloucester County, Virginia, chose as its preacher William Lemon, a black.[64]

But the case of Jacob Bishop, a slave preacher from Northampton County, Virginia, is more revealing. According to Baptist historian Lemuel Burkitt, around 1795 the "brethren and friends in that county gave him [Bishop] money to buy his freedom, which he did, and soon after bought his wife's. And when he came to Norfolk he bought his eldest son's freedom. His preaching was much admired both by saints and sinners, for sometime, wherever he went." However, white Baptists from neighboring associations soon decided "that whereas the black brethren in the church seemed anxious for a vote in conference, that it would be best to consider the black people as a wing of the body, and Jacob Bishop to take the oversight of them, as this church, at that time consisted of a number of blacks." At first the blacks "seemed pleased," but they subsequently told the deacons that such segregation was "dishonoring to God, and said they would be subordinate to the white brethren. . . ." So the white and black associations were reunited, but this time under a white minister.[65] Blacks in the most fundamental sense had asserted their belief in equality and in their dignity as men. Pressure for segregation of the races because of rising tensions—for reasons which will be explored more fully in the last chapter—ultimately prevailed, however. By 1811 segregated seating was instituted in several Baptist churches, and even a wooden partition was built between the races, much to the distress of the black brethren.[66]

The gains and opportunities offered by the Methodists and Baptists notwithstanding, religion was still too often another instrument of social control for slaveholders. The manner in which Joshua Freeman, an eastern North Carolina planter, utilized religion to exact acceptable behavior from his slaves demonstrates this point. "Although he had many slaves," one Baptist historian explained, "his lenity towards them was very remarkable. If any of them transgressed, his general method to chastise them was to expose their fault before the rest of his servants and the whole family, when they came in to family worship in the morning: who, when assembled at morning prayer, would talk to them, exhort and rebuke them so sharply for their faults, that made others fear."[67]

Repelled ultimately by the brand of religion their masters expounded, Afro-Americans colored their religion in ways that related most directly to their experience. Discreet worship meetings in the Negro quarters or some secluded arbor displaced the masters' institutionalized religion. Moreover, though the 1715 slave code barred Negroes from holding their own religious services, blacks were worshiping separately by 1800. The enforced segregation, however, allowed slaves to express unabashedly their longings for freedom. Nonetheless some caution had to be exercised as in the case of one old slave preacher who, in the presence of a white observer, became carried away and exclaimed: "Free indeed, free from death, free from hell, free from work, free from white folks, free from everything." In the slaves' religion, then, certain Bible stories took on additional meaning, spirituals carried hidden messages, and Afro-Americans worshiped a God who they prayed would some day free them:[68]

> O my Lord delivered Daniel
> O why not deliver me too?

CHAPTER IV

Wars of Liberation

The American Revolution was in many respects a colonial war for independence. Subjected to increasingly meddlesome imperial regulations after the 1740s, American colonials took up arms to fight for their liberation.[1] Yet if some white Americans were moved by the ideology of the Revolution and the eloquent prose of Jefferson's Declaration of Independence, few equated the struggle with black liberation. Afro-Americans, however, had another view. Whether as patriots or tories, Negroes saw the Revolution as an unprecedented opportunity for freedom. The political ideologies of the two sides had less importance for Afro-Americans than the goal of freedom. Indeed, historians have tended to lionize black patriots such as Crispus Attucks—slain at the Boston Massacre in 1770—when the evidence suggests that those blacks who took action in the Revolution were more likely to join the British.[2] The American Revolution, then, had complexities often overlooked by historians but all too real for eighteenth-century Americans. In short, two wars of liberation were taking place concurrently in which black and white objectives sometimes converged but just as often diverged.

Though the revolutionaries tried to ignore the problem of holding a large, enslaved populace in check while waging a war, British authorities, events, and Afro-Americans themselves conspired to thrust the question of the slaves' disposition to the center of political and especially military debates. As early as 1773, before the war had begun, one British observer offered this military evaluation of the South: "The Southern Provinces may be entirely thrown out of the Question, not only as being thinly peopled & enervated, But from the great Majority of Negroes intermixed, which exposes them to immediate ruin whenever we detach a small Corps to support an Insurrection."[3] Not unmindful of the threat of a slave revolt, southern revolutionaries were convinced that the British meant to foment a genuine social upheaval to squelch colonial agitation for independence. Joseph Hewes, a North Carolina delegate to the Continental Congress, wrote urgently in the summer of 1775 that the British intended "to let loose Indians on our Frontiers, [and] to raise the Negroes against us. . . ." The scheme allegedly included the arming of slaves.[4] Contemplating the causes of the Revolution in June, 1776, James Iredell denounced Britain's "diabolical purpose of exciting our own Domestics (Domestics they forced on us) to cut our throats, and involve Men, Women and Children in one universal Massacre. . . ."[5]

During the opening stages of the Revolutionary War, as rumors of an imminent slave rebellion swept the South, the various revolutionary bodies took measures to control the black population. In 1774 the North Carolina Provincial Congress resolved: "We will not import any slave or slaves, nor purchase any slave or slaves imported or brought into this province by others from any part of the world. . . ."[6] This resolution has generally been interpreted as a strong statement of principle in order to show the British that all forms of trade would be boycotted. And indeed on at least two occasions the committee of safety in the Lower Cape Fear enforced the measure by reshipping slaves brought in by water. But it may also have had a practical intent. Since newly imported slaves from Africa or the West Indies tended to be the most rebellious, Carolina slaveholders doubtless wished to avoid compounding an already unstable situation with troublesome newcomers. The Wilmington Committee of Safety, for instance, ordered five Negroes brought from the West Indies in December, 1774, reshipped immediately, but when Cornelius Harnett, the committee's leader, asked to import a slave from Rhode Island whom he had purchased before the nonimportation agreement, the committee unanimously allowed the exception.[7]

Revolutionaries nervously monitored the slave population. The Wilmington committee in June, 1775, insisted that all blacks be disarmed so as to keep the "Negroes in order," and it instituted "Patroles to search for & take from Negroes all kinds of Arms whatsoever, & such Guns or other Arms found with Negroes shall be delivered to the Captain of the Company of the District. . . ." Moreover, when the committee ordered that all citizens take an oath of allegiance to the Revolutionary regime, it also asserted "that no master shall prevent his apprentices or servants" from signing the association. Wilmington's patriots believed their situation "truly alarming, the Governor collecting men, provisions, warlike stores of every kind, spiriting up the back counties, & perhaps the Slaves. . . ."[8]

Overpowering anxieties gripped Wilmington in the summer of 1775. The revolutionaries charged that John Collet, the British commander at Fort Johnston, "had given Encouragement to Negroes to Elope from their Masters & they [the British] promised to protect them."[9] Martial law was imposed to control loyalists and blacks. Janet Schaw, then visiting the Lower Cape Fear, watched the mounting hysteria. According to her, the revolutionaries were claiming that the crown had promised "every Negro that would murder his Master and family that he should have his Master's plantation. This last Artifice they may pay for, as the Negroes have got it amongst them and believe it to be true. Tis ten to one they may try the experiment, and in that case friends and foes will be all one."[10]

When Mrs. Schaw traveled to Wilmington, the slaves accompanying her "were seized and taken into custody till I was ready to return with them." An insurrection was expected hourly. "There had been a great number of them [blacks] discovered in the adjoining woods the night before," she explained, "most of them with guns, and a fellow belonging to Doctor [Thomas] Cobham was actually killed. All parties are now united against the common enemies." Every white man was armed, and searches of Negro houses took place regularly. The town was patrolled day and night; a curfew of 9:00 P.M. had been set for blacks.[11]

Mrs. Schaw remained suspicious. A thoroughgoing loyalist, she talked to the commander of the midnight patrol who "believed the whole was a trick intended in the first place to inflame the minds of the populace, and in the next place to get those who had not before taken up arms to do it now and form an association for the safety of the town." As for the death of Cobham's slave, "it was a fact well known" that he met his "Mistress every night in the opposite wood." Because her master was so strict, she was forced "to carry on the intrigue with her black lover with great secrecy. . . ." Even so, Mrs. Schaw felt "that the Negroes will revolt."[12]

As in many other instances, it is difficult to separate black conspiracies from white fantasies of slave insurrection. But the fears of the Carolina slaveholders were not groundless. Royal Governor Josiah Martin, who was then formulating plans for a massive British invasion of the South beginning in North Carolina, did not entirely dismiss the idea of arming slaves. He wrote the Earl of Dartmouth in June, 1775: "Although Virginia and Maryland are both very populous, the Whites are greatly outnumbered by the Negroes, at least in the former; a circumstance that would facilitate exceedingly the Reduction of those Colonies who are very sensible of their Weakness arising from it."[13] Then in a letter to Lewis DeRossett which fell into the hands of the revolutionaries and became public, Martin stated that he had never advocated a slave revolt except in the case of "the actual and declared rebellion of the King's subjects, and the failure of all other means to maintain the King's Government."[14]

Whatever Martin's intentions, a slave uprising apparently did occur in July, 1775, along a crescent from Beaufort through Pitt and Craven counties. On July 8, the Pitt County Safety Committee ordered out patrollers to "shoot one or any number of Negroes who are armed and doth not willingly surrender their arms, and that they have Discretionary Power, to shoot any Number of Negroes above four, who are off their Masters Plantations, and will not submit."[15] The insurrection, supposedly originating in Beaufort County, was termed "a deep laid Horrid Tragick Plan laid for destroying the inhabitants of this province without respect of persons, age or sex." A posse of some one hundred men apprehended the "suspected heads" of the plot until over forty blacks had been jailed. The movers behind the scheme were said to be a white sea captain and "Merrick, a negro man slave who formerly Belonged to Major Clark a Pilot at Okacock but now to Capt Nath Blinn of Bath Town. . . ." Five Negroes were whipped, several of whom received "80 lashes each" and had their ears cropped.

No sooner had those blacks been punished than word came of other Negroes "being in arms on the line of Craven and Pitt. . . . We posted guards upon the roads for several miles that night." Another report held that a body of 250 blacks had been pursued for several days "but none [was] taken nor seen tho' they were several times fired at." According to the Negroes captured, the plan was for the slaves to rise up as one on July 8 and "to fall on and destroy the family where they lived, then to proceed from House to House (Burning as they went) until they arrived in the Back Country where they were to be received with open arms by a number of Persons there appointed and armed by Government for their Protection, and as a further reward they were to be settled in a free government of their own." The fact that the white patrollers in "disarming the negroes" recovered "considerable ammunition" lends credence to the probability that some North Carolina blacks, as Janet Schaw observed, did believe the British would provide them with a "free government" if they revolted.[16]

One of the more curious aspects of this putative slave rebellion is the leadership role ascribed to Merrick, evidently a Negro pilot.

Pilots were absolutely critical to coastal trade in colonial America, and nowhere more so than North Carolina with its hazardous shallows and swirling currents. As noted earlier, tensions existing between black and white pilots erupted in 1773. Now with pilots potentially assuming crucial military functions as the threat of war and invasion loomed, black pilots became all the more suspect. In Charlestown in August, 1775, less than a month after the North Carolina rising, revolutionaries executed a free Negro named Thomas Jeremiah, a pilot and reputed loyalist said to be inciting the slaves to revolt. White Carolinians' suspicions about black pilots soon became prophecy, for the British employed black pilots throughout the war.[17]

Such conspiracies as those discovered in North Carolina and Charlestown were probably doomed to failure because the blacks involved had limited opportunities to organize effectively, a paucity of arms, and little hope of succeeding without outside support. Virginia's royal governor—John Murray, Earl of Dunmore—quickly promised that support, however. On November 7, 1775, Lord Dunmore from aboard the *William* in Norfolk harbor announced that "all indented servants, Negroes, or others, (appertaining to Rebels,) [are] free, that are able and willing to bear arms, they joining His Majesty's Troops, as soon as may be, for the more speedily reducing the Colony to a proper sense of their duty, to His Majesty's crown and dignity."[18]

The reaction in the black communities of Virginia and North Carolina was electric. Almost immediately some three hundred Negroes joined Dunmore's forces. Other bondsmen rushed toward Norfolk to fight for the British. The slave Charles, "a very shrewd sensible fellow" who could read and write, defected. His master asserted: "From many circumstances, there is reason to believe he intends an attempt to get to lord *Dunmore*. . . . from a determined resolution to get liberty. . . ."[19] Twelve Negroes, termed "Dunmore's banditti," invaded one plantation, robbed the owner of all his valuables, and carried off two Negro women. Another report stated: "Nine Negroes (two of them women) who had been endeavouring to get to Norfolk in an open boat and put ashore on Point Comfort, were fired upon by some persons in pursuit, taken, and brought here on Thursday; two of the fellows are wounded, and it is expected the rest will soon be made example of."[20] Likewise a "Tory colonel . . . enlisted 300 slaves and convicts, but was defeated and obliged to fly to lord Dunmore. . . ."[21]

By December, 1775, the Virginia governor had dubbed his black

By His Excellency the Right Honorable JOHN Earl of DUNMORE, His Majesty's Lieutenant and Governor General of the Colony and Dominion of Virginia, and Vice Admiral of the same.

A PROCLAMATION.

AS I have ever entertained Hopes, that an Accommodation might have taken Place between GREAT-BRITAIN and this Colony, without being compelled by my Duty to this most disagreeable but now absolutely necessary Step, rendered so by a Body of armed Men unlawfully assembled, firing on His MAJESTY's Tenders, and the formation of an Army, and that Army now on their March to attack His Majesty's Troops and destroy the well disposed Subjects of this Colony. To defeat such treasonable Purposes, and that all such Traitors, and their Abettors, may be brought to Justice, and that the Peace, and good Order of this Colony may be again restored, which the ordinary Course of the Civil Law is unable to effect; I have thought fit to issue this my Proclamation, hereby declaring, that until the aforesaid good Purposes can be obtained, I do in Virtue of the Power and Authority to ME given, by His Majesty, determine to execute Martial Law, and cause the same to be executed throughout this Colony; and to the end that Peace and good Order may the sooner be restored, I do require every Person capable of bearing Arms, to resort to His Majesty's STANDARD, or be looked upon as Traitors to His Majesty's Crown and Government, and thereby become liable to the Penalty the Law inflicts upon such Offences; such as forfeiture of Life, confiscation of Lands, &c. &c. And I do hereby further declare all indented Servants, Negroes, or others, (appertaining to Rebels,) free that are able and willing to bear Arms, they joining His Majesty's Troops as soon as may be, for the more speedily reducing this Colony to a proper Sense of their Duty, to His Majesty's Crown and Dignity. I do further order, and require, all His Majesty's Liege Subjects, to retain their Quitrents, or any other Taxes due or that may become due, in their own Custody, till such Time as Peace may be again restored to this at present most unhappy Country, or demanded of them for their former salutary Purposes, by Officers properly authorised to receive the same.

GIVEN under my Hand on board the Ship WILLIAM, off Norfolk, the 7th Day of NOVEMBER, in the SIXTEENTH Year of His Majesty's Reign.

DUNMORE.

(GOD save the KING.)

recruits "Lord Dunmore's Ethiopian Regiment." Emblazoned across the chest of each black's uniform was the bold legend: "Liberty to Slaves." With nearly two thousand men under his command, of whom about one-half were black, Lord Dunmore posed a serious threat to the Revolutionary movements in Virginia and North Carolina. Robert Howe with his Continental unit and minutemen from Edenton was immediately dispatched to Norfolk. The line of march of the North Carolina troops had a dual purpose: to block any move by Dunmore toward North Carolina, and to prevent the Negroes of Pasquotank, Currituck, and adjacent counties from flying to the British liberator.

The Battle of Great Bridge near Norfolk crushed the incipient British offensive in Virginia and quelled immediate fears of a servile insurrection. But many blacks had taken up arms to fight for their liberation. At one skirmish North Carolina troops encountered a "guard of about 30 men, chiefly negroes." According to one participant, "We killed one, burnt another in the house, and took two prisoners (all black). . . ." North Carolina patriots asserted that the defeat of the "Negroes and Tories" thwarted "an avowed Intention to seduce the Slaves of that Part of the Colony of Virginia, and the lower Parts of this Province, to revolt from their Masters."[22]

Still Dunmore's proclamation had clearly quickened slaves' hopes for freedom and produced a disturbing portent for southern slaveholders: blacks with a "determined resolution to get liberty" would join the British. Dunmore's impact on the black community could be measured by a report from New York that "a lusty NEGRO WENCH in Monmouth county was delivered of a male child, who, in memory of a certain notable NEGRO CHIEF, is named DUNMORE."[23]

In the light of these alarming trends the North Carolina patriots moved hastily to interdict the mass defection of Negroes to the British. The Fourth Provincial Congress in May, 1776, appointed a committee "to enquire of ways and means the most probably to prevent the desertion of slaves." Since the British were then raiding the Lower Cape Fear, the committee recommended that all slaveholders "on the south side of Cape Fear River . . . remove such male slaves as are capable of bearing arms, or otherwise assisting the enemy, into the country, remote from the Sea. . . ."[24]

But even inland other threats to slavery loomed. Antislavery sentiment in the Carolina backcountry was beginning to stir as certain dissidents, particularly Quakers, raised embarrassing questions about the peculiar institution by the 1770s. In 1774 the freeholders of Rowan County protested the slave trade with rare vehemence: "Resolved that the African slave trade is injurious to this colony, obstructs the population of it, prevents manufacturers and other useful emigrants from Europe from settling among us, and occasions an annual increase of the balance of trade against the colonies."[25] In fact, the General Assembly did impose an import tax on the slave trade in 1786, calling the commerce "productive of evil consequences and highly impolitic." But that tax was rescinded in 1790, giving the slave trade a free rein until ended by the federal Constitution in 1808.

The Rowan petitioners had scored slavery on the grounds that it provided unfair competition with white labor and discouraged the development of industry and European emigration. North Carolina Quakers, however, attacked the institution as abhorrent to the natural rights of man. Thomas Newby of Perquimans County, feeling "uneasy" about "keeping Negroes in bondage," asked the advice of the Quakers' Standing Committee of the Yearly Meeting. The committee advised Newby and other Friends to free their slaves. Going one step further, the Yearly Meeting ordered in 1775 that "no Friend in unity shall either buy or sell a Negroe without the Consent of the Monthly Meeting. . . ." At the height of the Revolutionary tumult in 1776 the Friends declared that, "Keeping our fellow men in Bondage is inconsistent with the Law of righteousness" and further stipulated "that all the members . . . who hold slaves be earnestly and affectionately advised to Cleanse their Hands of them as soon as they possibly can. . . ."[26]

Within the first year of this ruling, North Carolina Quakers liberated over forty slaves. Obviously angered by the Friends' actions, the General Assembly enacted a law in 1777 "to prevent domestic Insurrections." The lawmakers denounced the "evil and pernicious Practice of freeing Slaves in this State, [which] ought at this alarming and critical Time to be guarded against. . . ." The statute reiterated the 1741 slave code which vested only the county courts with the power of judging "meritorious Services" for the manumission of slaves. Furthermore, any slaves freed contrary to the law were to be apprehended and auctioned off by county sheriffs.[27] One white Carolinian contended that the law was necessary because the Quakers refused "to give Security that the Negroes shall not become Burthensome to the State."[28] But the intentions of the legislature were clear: newly freed slaves threatened the security of the Revolutionary regime.

Sheriffs immediately began rounding up recently freed blacks and selling them at public auctions. The Quakers protested that the 1777 act was operating *ex post facto* in violation of the English common law. The Standing Committee hired lawyers to contest the seizures but to no avail. In 1778 the General Assembly ruled that all sales of illegally freed slaves were bona fide with one exception: "any Slave who having been liberated & not sold by order of any Court has inlisted in the service of this [state] or the United States previous to the passing of this Act."[29] Thus, blacks joining the Revolutionary army before 1777 could retain their freedom.

Most of the blacks liberated by the Quakers remained in bondage, however. When Friends tried once more in 1779 to petition the legislature to repeal the laws of 1777 and 1778, a legislative committee said bluntly that "the Conduct of the said Quakers in setting their Slaves free, at a time when our open and declared Enemies were endeavoring to bring about an Insurrection of the Slaves, was highly criminal and reprehensible, and that it was also directly contrary to the known and Established Laws of the Country."[30] Through the years, nonetheless, the Quakers found ingenious ways in which to flout the law, as in the 1780s when Friends gave a number of slaves their quasi freedom by allowing them to keep the "full Benefit of their labour."[31]

Few North Carolina Negroes, however, could depend on the benevolence of Quakers or other whites to free them. What they could rely on was their own determination for freedom, service in the American or British cause, and the chaos and social dislocation spawned by the war. It was an opportunity that thousands of Afro-Americans seized.

CHAPTER V

In the Service of King or Country

Initial efforts by Afro-Americans to organize resistance to the Revolutionary movement by taking up arms or fighting for the British met fierce and swift retaliation in Virginia, North Carolina, and South Carolina in 1775-1776. The blacks' quest for freedom was undiminished, but greater caution and calculation had to be exercised. Moreover, not all blacks sided with the British. Many rallied to the American cause. Indeed, free blacks appear to have had a greater propensity for joining the Continental Line or state militia than the British army. Slaves, on the other hand, flocked to the British, in part because of the patriots' misgivings about arming them, and too because the British seemed to offer the better chance for freedom. In either case Afro-Americans provided significant manpower to both sides in the Revolutionary struggle.

After Lord Dunmore's proclamation in 1775, George Washington—commander of the Revolutionary army—moved to enlist free blacks to forestall them from joining the British. Earlier the Continental Congress and certain officers in the army had decided to bar the use of slaves or free blacks. But the brave efforts of black soldiers at Bunker Hill and other opening battles caused Congress to reverse its decision. South Carolina in particular resisted moves to arm Negroes, but the policy gained more and more support in the Upper South and North as the war dragged on. Only Maryland authorized slave enlistments and subjected free blacks to the draft, but many free blacks enlisted in the army or navy in Virginia and North Carolina as well as in other states, including Massachusetts, Delaware, and Connecticut. Perhaps as many as three-quarters of Rhode Island's Continental troops consisted of slaves who had been offered freedom for their service. In some instances slaves were permitted to serve as substitutes for their masters.[1]

When the British invaded the South in 1778-1779, the Congress empowered South Carolina and Georgia to raise 3,000 black troops for their defense. Although the blacks were to receive no bounty and be under the direction of white officers, they were to have their freedom at the end of the war. John Laurens, a Continental officer and the son of the prominent South Carolina patriot Henry Laurens, was given the task of convincing his state of the need for Negro troops. Nathanael Greene, commander of the Southern Army during the last two years of the war, believed strongly that black regiments should be formed. As late as 1782 he said that he was so "fully impressed with the practicability . . . and advantage of the measure that I cannot help working to see it attempted." South Carolina and Georgia, however, absolutely refused to entertain the notion. As the republican governor of Georgia explained to Greene: "the raising a body of blacks . . . will not go down with the people here. . . ."[2] In the end the plan for organized black regiments failed.

Nonetheless, hundreds of Negroes bore arms for the patriots. Negro combatants were interspersed with whites. At White Plains, New York, in August, 1778, the order was given for a "return of all the negroes in the several Regiments to be made Regimentally and digested into Brigade returns . . . specifying those present and the particular places those absent and on command are."[3] The return showed a total of fifty-eight Negroes in the North Carolina Line.[4]

It seems clear, however, that over the course of the war many more North Carolina blacks doubtless fought for the American cause. The problem in identifying them is that the records rarely made distinctions between "persons of colour" and whites. Some blacks continued to serve in the militia, but an unknown number enlisted in the Continental Line. Most of these blacks were free Negroes, though in a few instances some slaves served as substitutes for their masters.

The most notable example of this latter practice was the case of Ned Griffen. Griffen, "a man of mixed blood," was owned by William Kitchen, a soldier in the North Carolina Brigade. Shortly before the Battle of Guilford Court House in 1781, Kitchen deserted and would have been returned to service had he not sent Griffen in his place, for which he promised the Negro his freedom. However, upon Griffen's discharge after the war, Kitchen reneged and sold him to a slave owner in Edgecombe County. Griffen petitioned the legislature for his freedom. In 1784 the General Assembly passed a law freeing Griffen "forever hereafter" and enfranchising him.[5]

Clearly, Griffen's discharge "from the yoke of slavery" by the legislature for his military service was singular. Free blacks, on the other hand, joined the patriot side evidently to protect the unusual status they already enjoyed. Their experiences were not unlike those of white soldiers, though blacks were more likely to be delegated the menial labor or utilized for their skills. Many were employed as military laborers building fortifications, crafting weapons, making munitions, clearing roads, and shoeing horses. Others acted as spies or guides. Frequently, blacks served as musicians or servants to white officers. Before the Battle of Camden, General Horatio Gates ordered "All Batmen, Waiters &c. who are soldiers taken from the Line . . . forthwith to join their Respective Regiments, and Act with their Masters while they are on Duty."[6]

The danger and drudgery of army life, however, knew no color. Some North Carolina blacks served in the army for seven years and fought in many of the crucial battles in both the North and the South. David Burnet was a "war soldier in Blount's Company, and his waiter sometime," who enlisted in the Fifth Regiment but probably died at Valley Forge in 1778. John Day, a "man of colour" from Granville County, escaped that frozen hell "by taking a dose of physic" and then drinking "freely of spirits which caused his death. . . ." William Foster "was taken Prisoner at Charlestow[n], when the town was taken by the British" in 1780. Charles Hood, on the other hand, marched out of Charlestown before its surrender and later fought at Eutaw Springs. David Ivey joined the Tenth Regiment in 1777, suffered through Valley Forge, and served first as a drummer and then waggoner before his discharge in 1783. Job Lott defected to the American side: "he was a waggoner to the British army, came over to West Point & brought a wagon load of flour which he sold to the Americans and enlisted in the service of the Continental Line."[7]

In some instances, black veterans became local folk heroes. Isaac Hammond of Fayetteville was a fifer who served at least two years in the southern campaign and saw action at Eutaw Springs. He died in 1822, but his wife filed a pension application in 1849 with the federal government. One of the supporting letters stated: "I have a perfect recollection of old Isaac. He was a fifer . . . & was also a good fiddler at weddings & other merry makings, and was too much given to making himself merry . . . whether at the Cool Spring on muster day of the Independent Company or elsewhere." His father was a barber, and both parents were described as "Mulattoes or Mustees having no african blood in them." In close elections in Fayetteville the Hammonds could "frequently shape

In 1781 Baron Ludwig von Closen, aid-de-camp to French General Rocham-
beau, painted this watercolor of American soldiers bivouacked at White
Plains, New York. He recorded in his diary: "A quarter of them were Negroes,
merry, confident and sturdy." Unfortunately, the baron's diary in the Library
of Congress has been lost.

the result." As late as the 1850s "Isaac the fifer" remained a local
legend in Cumberland County.[8]

A number of North Carolina blacks also served in the naval
forces. When the Continental frigate *Randolph* captured four
vessels bound for New York from Jamaica in 1777, among the
crew was "one Mr. M'Queen, with several of his Negroes,"
volunteers from Wilmington.[9] The slave James of Perquimans
County made "Several Voyages from This State & Virginia"
during the war. On at least two occasions he was captured by the
British but "Embraced the Earliest Opportunity in Making his
Escape to Return to this Country." Because he had served on an
"American Armed Vessel," the county court granted him his
freedom.[10]

The Continental Army was not noted for its discipline, and the
black soldiers were no exception. Four "colored people Gears,
Billy, George and Jack" deserted from General Francis Nash's
regiment in 1776, shortly after the Battle of Moore's Creek.[11]
John Toney of Halifax fought at the Battle of Guilford Court
House, "ran home and was taken and made to serve to the end of
the war."[12] Both the patriot and British armies plundered
farmers of livestock and produce with little compunction. At the

height of the southern campaign one Moravian wrote with relief, "Two soldiers and eight negroes came from General [Daniel] Morgan's camp, were fed, and thankfully returned thither."[13] Joseph Hastings of Orange County was not so fortunate, however. Four "Black Persons being Soldiers, VIZT. Thomas Thompson, Leonard Turner, Valentine Murrin & John Adams" of the Maryland Line broke into Hastings's home, "unmercifully abusing him . . . , carrying away with them, in a felonious Manner, a large Sum of Gold & Silver Coin, with sundry Garments of Clothes. . . ." Before justice could be served, however, the black soldiers "were forcibly rescued from the Court, contrary to the Civil Law & Power of this State. . . ."[14] Evidently, the Maryland Line, generally regarded as one of the best fighting units in the Continental Army, was not willing to lose four of its men to a civilian court.

Not all Negroes served the patriot cause willingly. Under the confiscation acts of 1777 and 1779 the property of known loyalists could be seized, including slaves. But as a 1780 law observed, such seizures often occurred with "violence and barbarity" and under "pretence." Negro slaves had been "conveyed to distant parts," while others sold "in violation of law and justice."[15] The slave Jacob, belonging to the loyalist Thomas McKnight, was "sent to one of the back counties to the iron works, and run away from that place."[16] Indeed, county sheriffs were empowered to hire out confiscated blacks, and the legislature resolved in 1777 to employ Negroes "on the Iron Works in Chatham County on account of the public concerned therewith. . . ."[17] Other masters simply hired out their slaves to the state to make a profit. Robert Burton's slaves in Granville County moved provisions from wharves to the Continental Army in 1781 and 1782.[18] John Walker's slaves, however, took advantage of the situation. Walker lent five slaves for "the public service" to assist the deputy quartermaster of Wilmington in conveying public stores from town at the approach of the British in 1781. The slaves worked for some time but never returned. In a petition to the assembly in 1785 Walker demanded £750 in compensation.[19]

The Continental Army regularly utilized black labor in support of its military operations by the simple expedient of impressment. One officer wrote South Carolina partisan leader Andrew Pickens in June, 1781, "All the Negroes not claimed by the inhabitants whom you think fit for the Pioneer or waggon Service you will please send to Head Quarters." Similarly, Nathanael Greene ordered a subordinate "to repair to Augusta and collect as many of the Militia and Negroes as you can and employ them in demolishing the works upon the Savannah river."[20]

Slaves were also used as inducements to raise white troops for the Continental Line. The North Carolina legislature in 1780 offered soldiers signing on for three years "one prime slave between the age of fifteen and thirty years...." South Carolina offered even greater enticements—three slaves for three years' service. When Georgia and South Carolina slaveholders tried to sue for the recovery of their confiscated slaves after the war, the North Carolina assembly simply passed laws affirming the titles to the Negroes now held by North Carolinians.[21] James Madison's reaction to the use of slaves as bounties for recruits perhaps best summarized the practice: "would it not be as well to liberate and make soldiers at once of the blacks themselves as to make them instruments for enlisting white Soldiers? It wd. certainly be more consonant to the principles of liberty which ought never to be lost sight of in a contest for liberty...."[22]

Relatively few North Carolina Negroes apparently earned their freedom by fighting for the patriot cause. For those free blacks who joined the Revolutionary army there were pensions if they or their wives lived into the 1820s and 1830s or perhaps land warrants in Tennessee, though only a handful seem to have claimed them. Most of the lands set aside for black veterans were escheated to the University of North Carolina in the 1820s. The rewards for blacks aiding the American cause were uncertain at best. If making a wager on one's freedom, a southern black looked to the British.

Wherever the British appeared, slaves ran. Lord Dunmore's proclamation in November, 1775, inflamed black longings for freedom, and slaves came to believe that black emancipation was a British war policy. Writing John Hancock in 1777, Robert Howe bemoaned the South's defensive posture: "how various and extensive the necessary lines of defence are, how numerous the black Domesticks who would undoubtedly flock in multitudes to the Banners of the Enemy whenever an opportunity offered...."[23] Joseph Galloway, the Pennsylvania loyalist, wrote the Earl of Dartmouth in January, 1778: "The Negroes may be all deemed so many Intestine Enemies, being all slaves and desirous of Freedom."[24] Howe and Galloway were correct. When the British burned Brunswick Town, one rumor held that Howe's slaves had helped put the torch to the village.

As soon as the British fleet dropped anchor off the Cape Fear in early 1776, North Carolina slaves began to desert their masters. Captain George Martin, under the command of Sir Henry Clinton, organized the Negroes into a company of Black Pioneers, support troops which relieved British soldiers of such onerous duties as building fortifications, laundering clothes, cooking, and managing the horses and wagons. When first formed, the Negro unit, numbering fifty-four, provided valuable intelligence on the roads and waterways of North Carolina, South Carolina, and Georgia. The slave Morris, for instance, was from Town Creek and knew the road as far as Cross Creek "and above that the road from Virg ᵃ to Charlestown." Thomas Payne, owned by John Gerard, had worked on the Wilmington ferry and knew the road as far northward as New Bern and as far southward as Georgia. One runaway, named River, had fled from Charlestown. His owner was Arthur Middleton, one of South Carolina's signers of the Declaration of Independence.[25]

Not just the slaves of patriots defected. Lieutenant Isaac DuBois, making a loyalist claim for compensation from the British government after the war, declared that his slave London, a baker, "joined the Kings Troops at Cape Fear in North Carolina, was taken into the Service by Order of Sir Henry Clinton, and inrolled in a Company of Black Pioneers under the Command of Captain George Martin, by which Service the said Slave became intitled to his Freedom. . . ." Clinton had refused to release the tory's slave in March, 1776, because he was "desirous to complete the Company, but declared if any Accident happened to the Slave while in service, he should be paid for."[26]

John Provey, a free black, linked up with British forces off the Carolina coast in June, 1776. The black loyalist claimed that he "was settled in the Province of North Carolina, of which he is a native, at the Commencement of the late unfortunate Troubles in North America, that he took the first Opportunity of joining His Majesty's Troops under the Command of Sir Henry Clinton at Cape Fear, leaving all his Property behind him, and remained with the Army till its arrival at New York in 1776, when he was regularly Inlisted into a Company, stiled the Black Pioneers, with which he bore arms until the End of the War." In New York Provey built a house which he ultimately "was obliged to relinquish on Account of his Attachment to the British Government." His losses in North Carolina included a "small dwelling House," two horses, a small field of Indian corn and potatoes, a dozen fowl, a dozen ducks, and a bed and household furniture. Provey clearly risked his freedom and property to fight for the British.[27]

The admiralty muster rolls of the ships off the Cape Fear in 1776 often contain the names of Negroes who "deserted from the Rebels" or "fled for Protection."[28]

Fig. 1

List of Negroes, March 3, 1776, who fled to the HMS *Scorpion*

*Abraham	*Morris	Thom 3d
*Murphy	*Thom 2d	Richard
Dick 1st	*Ben	Presence
Thom 1st	*John 2d	Cato
John 1st	*Dick 2d	Maryann
Abberdeen	*Betty	Peggy
*Gilbert	Rose	Polly
*Goosman	Claranda	Grace
*Bobb	*Jacob	Dick 3d
*Friday	*James	Queen
*Quash	Arthur	Patience
Thena		
Peggy		
Jeffery		

The blacks assigned an asterisk joined Sir Peter Parker's fleet on May 21, 1776, for service in the Royal Navy. Several black refugees who boarded the HMS *St. Lawrence* off the Cape Fear in April, 1776, later joined the British army under Lord William Howe on Staten Island in New York harbor.[29]

The first opportunity for North Carolina blacks to defect to the British spanned a few brief months in the spring and summer of 1776. It was not until the British inaugurated a major southern offensive in late 1778 that black Carolinians in any sizable numbers could truly choose sides in the conflict. Indeed, for the first time since Lord Dunmore's daring attempt to foment a slave uprising, the British were pursuing an aggressive policy of enlisting the entire Negro population in a movement to crush the patriots' rebellion. On June 30, 1779, Sir Henry Clinton, commander of the British army in America, issued his Philipsburgh Proclamation in which he pledged "to every NEGRO who shall desert the Rebel Standard, full security to follow within these Lines, any Occupation which he shall think proper." Later Clinton even suggested that the emancipated blacks could be settled after the war on lands forfeited by the American rebels.[30]

The social disruption, internal dissension, and chaos of the southern war are only now beginning to be understood.[31] The war in the Carolina backcountry which exploded in 1779 and continued well into 1782 was exacerbated, to be sure, by the British army, but it was in many respects a civil, internecine conflict. Nathanael Greene pleaded with Andrew Pickens in 1781 to restrain the terrorism sweeping the backcountry. One whig band, he wrote, "plunders without mercy and murders the defenseless people just as private peak prejudice or personal resentments dictate." To Greene, who was ever sensitive to the political and social consequences of the war, the "idea of exterminating the Tories is not less barbarous than unpolitical."[32] A Wilmington correspondent informed Alexander Martin, North Carolina's acting governor, that the "depredations committed by the Western militia upon friends and foe are scarce to be parallelled. All Mr. Clayton's negroes and other movables are carried off as lawful plunder by those who never ventured their persons for any of it. . . . Several negroes and horses, the property of noted whigs, are also taken." Moreover, he continued, "Our negroes, going about our lawful business, and even in the Act of bringing fuel, without which we cannot exist in this season, are impressed, and all this is done without any warrant, or any Certificate given. . . ."[33] In this unstable situation the British forces beckoned the slaves like an army of liberation.

As the flames of war spread through Georgia and South Carolina and licked at the borders of North Carolina by 1780, whigs anxiously watched the overpowering attraction of the British for slaves. When the redcoats attacked Portsmouth, Virginia, in 1779, one whig fumed to North Carolina patriot Thomas Burke: "They got about 500 Negroes, & 100 whites were found base enough to enlist with them as soldiers." Another North Carolinian, Whitmel Hill, the state's largest slave owner, excoriated the British for "carrying off large droves of . . . Slaves [;] a very considerable number of them are brought into this State and sold."[34]

The blacks, however, needed little encouragement to fly to the British. In the words of Charles Stedman, Cornwallis's commissary officer, "The negroes in general followed the British army."[35] Indeed, Charles, Lord Cornwallis was determined to make the best possible use of the black refugees. So many slaves were beseeching his army as it drove north that the British commander had to develop deliberate plans for their utilization. At one point Henry Clinton even wrote to Cornwallis: "As to the Negroes, I will leave such orders as I hope will prevent the Confusion that would arise from a further desertion of them to us, and I will consider of some Scheme for placing those we have on abandoned Plantations on which they may subsist. In the mean time Your Lordship can make such Arrangements as will discourage their joining us."[36]

Instead of discouraging blacks, however, Cornwallis mobilized them to perform diverse assignments for his army. British officer Nisbet Balfour, poised on the North Carolina border, secured Ninety-Six by using Negroes to build the fortifications: "the loyal inhabitants are all willing to give their negroes, which with those of the rebells can very soon finish the business. . . . The Negroes belonging to Rebells . . . can sett about these redoubts." Balfour explained that, "Many Negroes captured from people who have left the country . . . are brought in here, I . . . mean to make use of some of them on the publick works. . . ."[37] Cornwallis instructed another subordinate to round up "one hundred able Negroes, furnished with Spades to be collected from the Plantations in your Neighborhood, and send them to Camden under an Escort of Militia."[38]

In September, 1780, Cornwallis appointed John Cruden, a North Carolina loyalist and merchant from Wilmington, "Commissioner of Sequestered Estates." Headquartered in Charlestown, Cruden eventually had responsibility for over 5,000 blacks on an estimated 400 rebel plantations. Cruden's job was to supplement the British army's commissary in the South by operating confiscated rebel plantations with the whigs' slaves. A year later Cruden's aegis was extended to North Carolina. Proclaimed Nisbet Balfour: "*Whereas* it has been represented to me that there are many Negroes the property of the Enemy within our Lines in North Carolina, which are now unemployed; In order therefore to prevent the said Negroes from becoming a burthen to Government or a nuisance to the Community *I do hereby* authorize and empower you to take the same into your custody and possession, and employ them to the best advantage, either in sawing lumber for the use of Colonel Moncrief in making Naval Stores, or in any other manner that may seem to you most advantageous to Govern-

Carolina blacks carefully watched the progress of the British army during the southern campaign and bolted for freedom when the redcoats approached. Kemble sketch from the *Century Magazine*, XXXI (1885-1886), 520.

ment. . . ."[39] In Charlestown alone Cruden employed Negroes in the Engineer's Department, Quartermaster General's Department, Barrack Master's Department, Commissary of Prisoners, Artificers, Drivers, Laborers, and General Hospital, including nurses.[40]

As he marched into North Carolina, Cornwallis and Charles Stedman skillfully utilized their Negro resources. Stedman collected provisions in the Carolina backcountry and operated several mills with 120 blacks, a sergeant, one cooper, and four overseers. By the opening of the campaign in North Carolina in January, 1781, Stedman had husbanded "50,000 weight" of meal packed and ready for use.[41] Cornwallis, meanwhile, turned his black legions into an army of foragers. Bands of Negroes numbering in the hundreds descended on Carolina farms and plantations, seizing livestock and stripping the residents of all food supplies. The commodities were turned over to regimental quartermasters, each of whom had eight Negroes to assist him in receiving provisions.[42]

To maintain order and discipline among the blacks, Cornwallis insisted that "all Negroes belonging to the Army" be marked so as to identify the regiment or department employing them. Any blacks not wearing the marks were to be flogged. Moreover, the deputy provost marshal was given "orders to Execute on the Spot any Negro Who is found quitting the Line of March in search of plunder." Cornwallis later ruled that no women or Negroes were to have horses.[43]

Nonetheless, the fervid blacks were not about to trade the strictures of their masters for the regulations of the British army. At Salisbury in February, 1781, Cornwallis expressed his outrage at reports of "the most Shocking Complaints of the Excesses Committed by the Troops. . . ." The British commander wanted to win the support of North Carolinians who harbored loyalist sentiments. Instead he received "Great Complaints . . . of Negroes Stragling from the Line of March, plundr[g] & Using Violence to the Inhabitants[.] It is Lord Cornwallis possitive Orders that no Negroe shall be Suffred to Carry Arms on any pretence. . . ." Cornwallis again reminded blacks of the deputy provost marshal's orders to shoot violators. Above all he demanded an end to the "Shamefull Marauding" and "Scandalous Crimes."[44]

The deeper Cornwallis drove into North Carolina, the more slaves deserted their masters. Lieutenant Colonel Hardy Murfree bluntly told Governor Abner Nash, "A great many Negroes goes to the Enemy."[45] According to one report, rebel slave owners were fleeing to Virginia "With their Negroes and Effects."[46]

Black Carolinians observed closely the progress of the British army, hung on rumors, and waited for the right moment to bolt for freedom. Mrs. Jean Blair wrote in January, 1781, while the main British columns were still a vast distance from eastern North Carolina, that, "The Negroes bring Strange storys. They say people are getting ready to run again and the English are to be in Edenton by Saturday." Once Cornwallis came in range, the trickle of runaways became a flood. "All my Brothers Negroes at Booth except two fellows are determined to go to them, even old Affra," said Mrs. Blair. "W [hitmel] Hill lost twenty in two nights." Mrs. Blair feared that the British and loyalists would not "visit the town" but rather the plantations along the waterways: "they will call along Shore for Negroes and other Plunder."[47]

Despite Cornwallis's putative concern for the zealotry of his black foragers, he never ceased using them. As the British army pushed from Wilmington toward Virginia, Mrs. Blair reported that everybody in Edenton was marching out "to surprise six hundred Negroes who were sent out by L Cornwallis to plunder and get provisions. It is said they have no Arms but what they find in the houses they plunder. When they applyed for arms they were told they had no occasion for any as they were not to go any place where any number of Rebels were collected. It is said there are two thousand of them out in different Partys."[48]

Further to the south Cornwallis had left Major James Craig in control of Wilmington. From the port city Craig launched numerous attacks as far north as New Bern. Craig used black coopers and sawyers "in the Public Works." He also seized rebels' slaves who had not flown to the British. One slaveholder reported the loss of "60 prime slaves." Another military leader feared that if Cornwallis returned to southeast North Carolina he could mobilize "500 Tories, and if he can arm them, 500 Negroes."[49]

When Craig evacuated Wilmington in November, 1781, some slaves escaped with the British while others remained by choice with their masters. William Hooper stated that, "Three fellows of mine had gone off with the British; one had been forced away by the militia, and I had lost five other negroes by the small-pox." His house slave John had resisted the British bribes. They offered him everything "to attach him to the service of the British"—clothes, money, freedom. "He pretended to acquiesce, and affected a perfect satisfaction at this change of situation; but in the evening of the day after Mrs. Hooper left the town, he stole through the British sentries, and without a pass, accompanied by a wench of Mrs. Allen's, he followed Mrs. Hooper seventy miles on foot, and overtook her, to the great joy of himself and my family." John's sister Lavinia, on the other hand, "pursued a different conduct. She went on board the [British] fleet after the evacuation of the town, and much against her will was forced ashore by some of my friends, and returned to me."[50]

Still the British army continued to attract Negroes like a magnet. At Yorktown Cornwallis put blacks to work on fortifications, for "the heat is too great to admit of the soldiers doing it...." In Portsmouth Benedict Arnold reported: "No time has been lost in repairing the old and erecting New Works here (in which the Negroes have been very serviceable) but none are yet compleat." When Virginia's republican Governor Thomas Nelson accused the British of seizing Negroes, Cornwallis replied: "No Negroes have been taken by the British Troops by my orders nor to my knowledge, but great numbers have come to us from different parts of the Country."[51]

For the most part blacks who joined the British performed noncombatant duties. Blacks who entered British service in 1775-1776 did in fact do some fighting in the northern states before 1778. However, in the last desperate days of the southern campaign the British turned to blacks for additional manpower along the battle lines. Black troops fought with the redcoats at Savannah in 1779. Two years later "the Rebel Partizan Sumpter [Thomas Sumter], made his long projected attack on the post of Congarees ... making many ineffectual attempts, in all which he was disgracefully beat off, and once by a small party of sequestered negroes."[52] Mrs. Blair asserted that at the Battle of Green Spring, fought near Jamestown, Virginia, in 1781, "The Negroes were at the Folly headed by some Refugee [tory] officers."[53] One American officer, commenting on the war in the Carolina backcountry, said: "the enemy oblige the negroes they have to make frequent sallies."[54]

Other blacks fought in the loyalist militia under such tory leaders as Samuel Bryan of Rowan County. Samuel Burke, a black loyalist, was credited with killing ten rebels at the Hanging Rock in August, 1780. A return of provincial troops in South Carolina and Georgia under Clinton at James Island in 1780 showed a detachment of guides and pioneers numbering ninety-two. Still other blacks served on privateers which clashed with patriot vessels and took them as prizes.[55] A number of black Continentals captured at the battles of Charlestown and Camden—and many more whites—enlisted in the British army for service in the West Indies with the Duke of Cumberland's Regiment of Carolina Rangers. At least six black pioneers for the rebels thus became soldiers of the crown in 1781: John Elliott, Jack, Thomas Blackmore, Tom (described as a drummer), Teas Horner, and Joseph Charles. The new recruits were to fight the Spanish; they received a bounty, clothing, and arms. Their new arrangement specified "that they are not expected at any time to fight against their Country men in America."[56]

As late as 1782 General Alexander Leslie pressed his superiors for permission to arm the Negroes at Charlestown against the expected assault by Greene's Southern Army. He wrote Clinton: "The necessity I shall in all probability be under of putting arms into the hands of negroes ... is it appears to me a measure that will soon become indispensably necessary shou'd the war continue to be carried on in this part of America." He also sought instructions on "what terms their freedom should be given them" for bearing arms. Indeed, a Negro cavalry unit clashed with American forces outside Charlestown in April, 1782, with two "Negro horse" soldiers losing their lives. Black contributions to the British war effort were aptly summed up by General William Phillips, who said: "These Negroes have undoubtedly been of the greatest use."[57]

With the surrender of Cornwallis at Yorktown in October, 1781, the disposition of the thousands of black refugees with the British became a source of grave concern to both the Americans and the British. The emancipation of blacks who had attached themselves to the British army had always been tenuous at best. British offers of emancipation during the war had been couched more in military exigencies than philosophical convictions. Indeed, many British officers had appropriated runaway blacks as property or given the rebels' slaves to loyalists to indemnify them for their losses. Nisbet Balfour had even suggested to Cornwallis in 1780 that twelve Negro prisoners of war taken at Camden be sold into slavery "to convince *Blacks* that he [*sic*] must not fight against us."[58]

Alexander Leslie explained his dilemma to Sir Guy Carleton. British officers, he said, "long in this country look on negroes as their property, and the slaves are exceeding unwilling to return to hard labour, and severe punishment from their former masters, and from the numbers that may expect to be brought off, including their wives, and children, if to be paid for, will amount to a monstrous expence." The officers "pretend them spyes, or guides, and of course obnoxious, or under promises of freedom from Genl. Prevost, Ld. Cornwallis, Ld. Rawdon, or some other officer of rank or free by proclamation." Leslie proposed to take only those blacks who had been paid for and put them to work for the "public service" in the West Indies. Unfortunately, "Genl. Green and their Governor [South Carolina's John Mathews] dont seem to agree in this business. . . ."[59]

Leslie's postscript was a neat understatement. The Americans were determined to prevent the mass exodus of blacks who had fled to the British. Though hundreds of loyalists were attempting to evacuate with their slaves, the focal point remained the thousands of blacks who had sought their freedom by joining the British. If protective of the loyalists' property, the British high command was not unsympathetic to the plight of black refugees. Said Leslie: "their number, which is very considerable, renders this a subject of much importance, and I am not a little embarrassed how to dispose of them." James Moncrief explained to Clinton that the "number of slaves who have attached themselves to the Engineer Department since my arrival . . . and who look up to me for protection has been for some time past a matter of serious concern." The British felt a moral obligation to these blacks. In Leslie's words, "There are many negroes who have been very useful, both at the Seige of Savannah and here; some of them have been guides, and from their loyalty been promised their freedom."[60]

Pressed by the rebel slave owners and diplomatic considerations on the one hand, and by the black fugitives themselves on the other, Leslie established a commission to hear appeals from both sides. His guiding policy was Clinton's Philipsburg Proclamation: those runaways who had served the army were to remain free. They would be removed to some other part of the empire and their owners compensated if they could prove their claims. All other blacks, chiefly those captured as prizes or sequestered on whig plantations, were to be returned to American claimants. Slaveholders were to be permitted to pass through British lines to find their Negroes without being "liable to any attack by your armed Parties," insisted Governor Mathews to General Leslie. However, before the final arrangements could be worked out, the two sides quarreled over disputed claims, Mathews withdrew his negotiators, and thus lacking American supervision thousands of blacks embarked on British ships when Charlestown was evacuated in late 1782. Perhaps as many as 5,000 black loyalists sailed from

Charlestown, many of them free, their destinations Jamaica, St. Augustine, New York, London, and Halifax.[61]

Meanwhile, in Paris and New York other diplomats debated the future of the black refugees. The commanders-in-chief of the American and British armies met in Orangetown, New York, in May, 1783, to discuss the fate of thousands of blacks still held by the British. According to the Provisional Peace Treaty, agreed upon in late 1782, the British were not to destroy or carry away "any Negroes or other Property of the American Inhabitants" during their withdrawal. But Sir Guy Carleton's interpretation of the treaty, much to General Washington's alarm, was that blacks already with the British before November 30, 1782, and who claimed freedom by the earlier proclamations should remain free and should not be considered American property. Carleton's defiant stand stilled mounting anxiety among the runaways in New York that they would be delivered up to their former masters. Boston King, a black Baptist preacher, recalled: "This dreadful rumour filled us all with inexpressible anguish and terror, especially when we saw our old masters, coming from Virginia, North-Carolina, and other parts, and seizing upon their slaves in the streets of New-York, or even dragging them out of their beds."[62]

In the end over 3,000 black loyalists evacuated New York. Carleton's "Book of Negroes," a register of the blacks under his supervision, listed a total of over 3,500 Negroes bound for Nova Scotia alone: 1,336 men, 914 women, and 750 children.[63] At least 8,300 blacks, moreover, were brought to East Florida from Savannah and Charlestown in 1782 and 1783. Many of these blacks, of course, remained the slaves of white loyalists. But a large number fled to the Indian country where they became black Seminoles—a process that had been going on for at least two centuries.[64] They would be heard from again in the Seminole wars of the nineteenth century.

The British policy at the end of the war had been genuinely forged from the fires of revolution. The disruption of southern society had enabled thousands of Afro-Americans to seek their freedom and in the most basic sense earn it in the service of the redcoats. To be sure, the policy had hinged on the honor of certain British officers—notably Moncrief, Leslie, and Carleton—and disputes with American officials had shrewdly helped to justify the black exodus. But it was the blacks themselves who forced the decisions by their persistent and unrelenting desire for freedom.

For those blacks who chose to stay behind or could not escape, the passions kindled by the American Revolution did not necessarily subside with the end of the war. The Revolution's aftermath brought tensions, not peace; and unrest, not passivity.

CHAPTER VI

Rising Tensions: The Impact of the Revolution

The close of the Revolutionary War in the South left the social arrangements of southern life in serious disarray. Thousands of Negro bondsmen had been lost to the British. Others had either earned their freedom or were simply claiming it. To rebuild the social structures which had prevailed before the war, southern whites moved quickly to redefine the status of blacks. This was accomplished in part by the escalation of the slave trade and natural increase among blacks as well. The black population of North Carolina grew faster during the 1790s than any other decade in the antebellum period. But the General Assembly also took measures to prevent manumissions and even to reenslave freed blacks. The conflict between the determination of white Carolinians to control blacks and Negro aspirations for freedom ineluctably led to rising tensions, culminating in the slave insurrection of 1802.

That blacks believed themselves heirs to the same promise the Revolution offered whites is perhaps best illustrated paradoxically by the extraordinary odyssey of a loyalist—Sergeant Thomas Peters of the Black Pioneers. Peters, a slave from the Lower Cape Fear, joined the British army in 1776 and evacuated New York with the British in 1783, his destination Nova Scotia. There he became a spokesman for the black loyalists, many of them from the Carolinas, who did not receive the land grants or fair treatment the British had promised. Representing over one hundred black families in Canada, Peters took his case to London. Secretary of State Henry Dundas ordered the colonial administrators of Nova Scotia and New Brunswick to fulfill the British pledge to the black loyalists by providing them with good lands. But the order was never carried out. Dundas also offered the disenchanted blacks an opportunity to migrate to Sierra Leone, a British colony in Africa. With prospects for better farms, equality as British subjects, their own government, and the complete abolition of slavery, some 1,200 black loyalists, led by Peters, settled in Africa. Though the black emigres never escaped white domination in Sierra Leone, they formed the nucleus of a modern

African state which even today traces in part its African nationalism from Negro American loyalists.[1]

Other black loyalists who fled to Nova Scotia in search of freedom suffered a much worse fate. In 1785 a ship from the Canadian province docked at New Bern. It evidently was manned by a number of Negro seamen and auxiliaries who had been slaves in North Carolina before the war, for upon learning of their presence the legislature passed a resolution asking the governor to secure the blacks on board. The lawmakers claimed that the Negroes were the property of United States citizens and that there was "a danger they may be secreted so that they may be lost to the owners. . . ." Governor Richard Caswell dispatched the following message to the sheriff of Craven County: "The Negroes brought into this place by Captain Gardner from Nova Scotia, which you have in custody, to-wit., Dominee, Peter, Zack, alias Digtry-Jacob, James Langly, Jim, Jack, Tom, Prince, Sam, Bett & Grace, you are required to retain in your Custody until you shall receive further orders. . . . And in the meantime you are to advertise in the public papers of Virginia, New York and this State the said Negroes describing each of them, and mentioning the names of the persons the said Negroes say they belong to. . . ." For these black loyalists freedom proved short-lived.[2]

Throughout the 1780s and 1790s countless free blacks were taken up by county sheriffs under the 1777 act to prevent "domestic insurrections." These Negroes were sold back into slavery for "passing as free Supposd. to have Been Mannumited by their former owners. . . ." A lawyer defending the Negro Judy before the Perquimans County Court submitted his reasons as to why reenslaving her was an error. The attorney asserted that Judy had been set free before 1777 and that "the taking apprehending and dragging of Negroes (as confessedly done in the Case) living quietly and peaceably with their masters from their houses, is arbitrary and illegal." Resorting to a natural rights philosophy, the counselor termed such practices "unjust & incompatible with liberty"; that they violated the Bill of Rights; and that "all Men possess certain natural & unalienable rights to life Liberty & property."[3] This remarkable defense of natural rights for a Negro must have inspired blacks as much as it disconcerted slaveholding whites.

Indeed, North Carolina seemed to be plagued by an epidemic of illegal manumissions in the aftermath of the Revolution. By 1790 North Carolina was the only state in the South where manumis-

Under a 1777 statute governing "domestic insurrections," many freed blacks were reenslaved during and after the Revolution. This document, dated October, 1788, is from the Perquimans County Slave Papers in the State Archives.

sion was not a slaveholder's prerogative. That power still rested with the county courts which had to adjudge "meritorious service." The restrictive law was passed again in 1788 and 1796. In one case the legislature even overturned the will of Mark Newby, who had intended that his slaves be freed at the age of twenty-one. His heirs, however, contested the will, and the assembly "from motives of justice and equity" confirmed the heirs' title to the slaves. Six assemblymen attacked the decision as "tyrannic and unconstitutional" because it unjustly deprived the blacks in question of their liberty.[4]

The Quakers' agitation for manumission continued to be the source of much of the lawmakers' consternation. During the last two decades of the eighteenth century the Quakers introduced numerous bills in the General Assembly calling for an end to the slave trade and the emancipation of all slaves. Nor was it any secret that the Quakers were the perpetrators of many illegal manumissions. A grand jury in Pasquotank County in 1795 angrily denounced the Quakers for subjecting the state to such

84

"great perril and danger." It expressed horror that "the idea of emancipation, amonghts Slaves is publicly held out to them, and incouraged by the Conduct of the Quakers; That the Minds of the Slaves, are not only greatly corrupted and allienated from the Service of Their Masters, . . . But runaways are protected, harbored, and incourag'd by them—Arsons are even committed, without a possibility of discovery."[5] Nathaniel Macon, North Carolina's archconservative congressman, stated in a 1797 debate on a Quaker petition concerning reenslaved Negroes that, "there was not a gentleman in North Carolina who did not wish there were no blacks in the country. It was a misfortune—he considered it a curse; but there was no way of getting rid of them. Instead of peace-makers, he looked upon the Quakers as warmakers, as they were continually endeavoring in the Southern States to stir up insurrections amongst the negroes."[6]

The Quakers, however, were not the only ones infected with the contagion of liberty and Revolutionary philosophy of natural rights. The two decades after the American Revolution witnessed widespread slave discontent both at home and abroad. The great Negro insurrections in the West Indies—especially the one in Saint-Domingue beginning in 1791—rang like a shrill alarm throughout the American South. Moreover, northern states were eradicating slavery—if not racial prejudice—as abolitionist societies sprang up on both sides of the Mason-Dixon line. The Pasquotank grand jury encapsulated these fears in its bitter denunciation of the Quakers who persisted in freeing slaves in spite of the "miserable havock and massacres which have taken place in the West Indies, in consequence of emancipation; Knowing the opinion of the Northern States; of the many thousand Slaves around them; and of the infatuated enthusiasm of Men calling themselves religious. . . ."[7]

The grand jury's anxieties seemed justified. Slave unrest pervaded North Carolina during the 1790s. A report from New Bern in 1792 asserted: "The negroes in this town and neighborhood, have stirred a rumour of their having in contemplation to rise against their masters and to procure themselves their liberty; the inhabitants have been alarmed and keep a strict watch to prevent their procuring arms; should it become serious, which I don't think, the worst that could befal[l] us, would be their setting the town on fire. It is very absurd of the blacks, to suppose they could accomplish their views. . . ."[8] Faced with mounting black assertiveness, the town commissioners of Fayetteville in 1797 authorized constables to administer fifteen lashes to "negroes that shall make a noise or assemble in a riotous manner in any of the streets on the Sabbath day; or that may be seen playing ball on that day." The legislature ordered free Negroes not to entertain slaves at their houses on the sabbath or after dark.[9]

In the summer of 1795 Wilmington suffered sporadic attacks by a "number of runaway Negroes, who in the daytime secrete themselves in the swamps and woods" and at night commit "various depredations on the neighboring plantations." They fatally ambushed at least one white overseer and wounded another. Posses eventually killed five of the renegades, including their leader known as the "General of the Swamps," and captured and executed four others, while several more remained at large.[10] When French refugees, fleeing the racial wars of the West Indies, sailed into Wilmington later in the year carrying thirty or forty of their slaves, residents prevented their landing, fearing that the West Indian blacks might incite an insurrection.[11] Indeed, Governor Samuel Ashe in 1798 issued a proclamation urging citizens to bar the landing of any Negroes, slave or free, from the West Indies; Ashe called on all civil and military officers on the coast to enforce stringently the slave trade laws.[12]

In this unsettled atmosphere every sign of slave rebelliousness spawned fears of a Negro revolt. In Bertie County in 1798 three black men were accused of leading a conspiracy of 150 slaves, armed with "Guns, clubs, Swords, and Knives." Evidently, the blacks "did attack, pursue, knock down and lay prostrate the patrollers" which resulted only in the death of a horse. Consequently, the three were found guilty of that charge, not rebellion, and punished with thirty-nine lashes and cropped ears.[13]

The trial of Quillo in Granville County, however, disclosed some disturbing attitudes and ideas within the slave community. In April, 1794, Quillo, the slave of James Hunt, was accused of plotting an insurrection. Slaves who testified against Quillo said that he "intended to give a large treat at Craggs Branch to the black people." While serving the blacks cider and brandy, Quillo planned to hold an "election" in which slaves would choose burgesses, justices of the peace, and sheriffs "in order to have equal Justice distributed so that a weak person might collect his debts, as well as a Strong one. . . ." These black authorities, representing the slaves, presumably might use force "in collecting the monies due them." Indeed, Quillo asked several slaves to present themselves as candidates.

Quillo's "election" may have been a cover for some deeper scheme. Certainly the resourceful slave had shown a fundamental belief in equal justice, and the fact that he went about organizing his polls with a "treat" in the same manner as a country squire standing for election to the General Assembly could not have been lost on local whites. Quillo had obviously imbibed deeply of democratic practices and philosophy, not just brandy and cider.

In his defense Quillo asserted that the idea for an election had come from a mulatto slave named Tom. The election had been called off because somebody had broken into one Mr. Smith's cellar and stolen liquor. If the election had been held, those slaves attending could have been charged with theft. The voting had therefore been postponed until the spring. Quillo had also been in touch with a Negro in Person County who had heard of a rising of Negroes intending to march toward Granville. One deponent charged that after the election Quillo "together with his associates were to proceed to inlist what forces they could to join the said party from Person and with them to force their way wherever they choosed, and to murder all who stood in their way, or opposed them." If the white people tried to interfere, Quillo vowed to "clear them out."[14]

If Quillo's election meant to combine bullets with ballots, it had been thwarted before any celebrant or insurgent tasted the liquor. Instead slave unrest in post-Revolutionary North Carolina reached a climax in 1802. The slave insurrection scare of that year was not isolated to one county or even one region. Reports of slave discontent centered in eastern counties like Camden, Bertie, Currituck, Martin, Halifax, Pasquotank, Hertford, Washington, and Warren, but others reached as far inland as Wake County and as far west as Charlotte.

The slave insurrection of 1802 in many respects culminated social and political developments that had been taking shape for several decades. The conspiracy came in the midst of the Second Great Awakening which was then enveloping the South. As shown earlier, religion was a powerful force in the slave community which released pent-up emotions and inspired black dreams of freedom. When mixed with the sense of equality fostered by the fellowship and brotherhood of evangelical Protestantism, the results proved explosive. Moreover, for over a decade slave rebellions had continued to erupt throughout the Western Hemisphere. In 1800 Gabriel Prosser, a blacksmith, had led a slave revolt in

Richmond, Virginia. The white backlash against initiatives for emancipation in the Revolution's aftermath, furthermore, had heightened tensions between the black and white communities. All these forces came to a head in 1802.

The insurrection scare itself seems to have been the product of one well-conceived plot in eastern North Carolina and perhaps several ancillary conspiracies in counties reaching deep into Virginia where similar rumors shook the Old Dominion. A principal leader was Tom Copper, who styled himself the "General to command this county in a plot to kill the white people. . . ." Copper had a camp hidden in the swamps near Elizabeth City. He evidently executed the most dramatic sortie of the insurrection when "six stout negroes, mounted on horseback" made a daring raid on the jail in Elizabeth City to liberate the slaves held there. Four were captured, but two escaped.[15]

The crux of the plot, however, was to be a massive uprising by the slaves on June 10, 1802. The blacks who organized the scheme included a critical number who could read and write, and hence pass information and messages, and several religious leaders who could reach a large audience by preaching to the various slaves on numerous plantations. In the latter instance the Great Revival thus became an opportunity for and an instrument of rebellion. Similarly, the Negroes used other social occasions such as a "Ball" to map out their strategy.

The Great Revival arrived in North Carolina in the fall of 1801. By early 1802 blacks and whites had been swept up in the emotional camp meetings and religious gatherings which bordered on hysteria. The Reverend Samuel McCorkle described how "as if by an electric shock, a large number in every direction, men, women, children, white and black, fell and cried for mercy. . . ." At one meeting "a stout negro-woman, who had been all day mocking the mourners, fell," McCorkle recorded, "and fell in a state of horror and despair that baffles description. . . . Two stout negro-men were no match for her struggles."[16]

More than pious conversions, however, were taking place at these religious gatherings. At one sermon the slave Charles angrily told another slave that "there were a great many whites there. . . . [and] that they ought to be killed. . . ." One master, who may have been a Baptist elder, gave the slave Virginia permission "to hold a night Meeting on Monday Night" at which plans for the revolt were subsequently discussed. The slave Moses admitted that "Joe Preached with a pistol in his pocket." Another slave alleged that at religious services she had observed several con-spirators "talking low" and "while at preaching saw [a] number of Negroes standing talking two & two during the sermon." The slave Frank, one of the ringleaders who was ultimately executed, had been seen at a "quarterly Meeting at Wiccacon. . . ." Apparently, the plotters planned to coordinate the rising with the quarterly meetings of several Kehukee Baptist associations when the whites would be most vulnerable. One insurgent stated that, "They were to begin at the Quarterly Meeting."[17]

Suspicious of the activities of various slave preachers, the Pasquotank County Court tried Dr. Joe in May, 1802, for con-spiring with Tom Copper "to Rebel and make insurrections." Dr. Joe, a slave preacher and physician, pleaded not guilty, and the jury refused to convict him. But his master had to post a bond of £200 for his release from jail plus two sureties of £250 each to guarantee Joe's good behavior. Moreover, the court enjoined the slave preacher not to "Assemble or hold any Meeting, Congrega-tion or other Assembly of Slaves or other people of Colour upon or under pretence of Preaching praying or exhorting or upon or under any other pretence Whatsoever."[18] Dr. Joe, perhaps one of the conspiracy's chief instigators, escaped the punishment which befell scores of other slaves.

The immediate causes of the rebellion remain obscure, but ac-cumulated tensions and grievances and the example of Gabriel Prosser's revolt apparently played a large part. Caesar, one of the leaders or "captains" of the cabal, told Moses that he foresaw "a Warm Winter, a dry Spring & a Bloody Summer, & that he expected the Negroes were going to Rise. . . ." Dave, another leader ultimately executed, confided to Sam that he was "very tired & weary" because "the Damn'd White people plagued him so bad they ought all to be killed & shall . . . if he could get a great many to join him. . . ." Peter "had fallen out with his overseer & had been whipped & Damn him he ought to be killed & all the rest." Peter had also attended "a logg roling & the Overseer had been whiping two of the negroes" which reinforced his determina-tion to revolt. Sam told Harry "that them guns we heard was in Virginia & that the Negroes was then fighting the White people. . . ." Indeed, Dave insisted the conspirators "could get encouragement from Virginia. The head negroes in Virginia lives about Richmond."

Several literate slaves set up a network of communication. As early as February, 1802, William R. Davie, the former governor

Governor Benjamin Williams was warned as early as February, 1802, that a slave insurrection might be brewing in the eastern counties. This portrait (artist unknown) is from the collection in the Museum of History.

and Revolutionary leader, had learned of a possible plot originating ironically in Southampton County, Virginia, and extending down the Roanoke River valley of North Carolina. In several letters to Governor Benjamin Williams, Davie compared the situation with Saint-Domingue where "the whole Colony" had been stained with the murder of several thousand whites. A printed circular letter had been found, supposedly written by a Negro organizing the revolt. The letter was addressed to the "Representative of the Roanoak Company" and stated that once the "conflagration" began whites would "acknowledge liberty & equality" and be "glad to purchase their lives at any price." Whites must learn that "the breath of liberty is as free for us as for themselves." The letter was signed by a "true friend in liberty or death."[19]

In June, 1802, while searching Negro houses, white militiamen near Colerain in Bertie County found a letter which began, *"Captain Frank Sumner is to command* (and then names of the men, and the 10th of June was the time) *you are to get as many men as you can—To Capt. King, Brown, &c."* The Negroes implicated in the letter were apprehended; Frank was executed; "a second was cropped, branded and whipped; a third was cropped and whipped, and the remainder whipped; there appearing

90

Eastern North Carolina, particularly the counties bordering the Albemarle Sound, was the scene of a major slave insurrection scare in 1802. Segment of the Price-Strother map (1808) from W. P. Cumming, *North Carolina in Maps* (Raleigh, 1966), plate 9.

nothing against them only their names being on the paper."[20]

This particular letter had evidently circulated throughout the northeastern counties in order to coordinate the timing of the rebellion. The Negro Dennis, owned by Thomas Fitts of Bertie County, confessed that Jacob in Perquimans County "Gave a letter to Mr. Browns Frank They all knew of This letter, he saw Jacob of Edenton & he told this depont. he Gave a letter to Frank, to be Carried to King who was to Carry it to Dave, Mr. Browns Hestor read the letter, & Said to Dave, Mr. Fitt & Mr. Brown was To be first Killed, as they were Supposed to be the head Men on The river."

The blacks reportedly cached guns and ammunition in the swamps and crafted other weapons such as clubs with nails driven through them. According to the plan as reconstructed by white interrogators, on the night of the rising the insurgents were to form into companies under their respective captains, "go to every man's house, set fire to it, kill the men and boys over 6 or 7 years of age; the women over a certain age, both black and white were to share the same fate; the young and handsome of the whites they were to keep for themselves, and the young ones of their own

91

colour were to be spared for waiters." The black rebels were then to converge on Plymouth "where they expected to receive considerable reinforcements from up and down the [Roanoke] river. . . . Some were offered county money to join, other[s] clothes and arms to go to Virginia to help the blacks there to fight the whites." Rumors of various black risings were rampant, but in at least one instance it appears that a band of rebels embodied near Windsor in Bertie County and marched toward the Roanoke River. In Washington County, meanwhile, another "rumpus" resulted in the shooting of "6 or 7 blacks . . . on their way to Williamston," which is also on the Roanoke.[21] Their more immediate objective may have been Plymouth and the linking of forces with the Bertie group.

Whether or not certain of the black insurgents truly contemplated replacing their white masters, taking white wives, and keeping black servants is difficult to determine. If so, these conspirators lacked the cohesiveness and nationalistic urgings of the blacks who had revolted in 1775-1776, or those Negro loyalists who migrated to Canada and then to Sierra Leone. On the other hand, whites may have been projecting their own guilt about the sexual abuse of black women onto the motives of the rebels. But as Michael Mullin has demonstrated, patterns of acculturation or creolization instilled values in Afro-Americans which set them apart from "new Negroes"—those recently imported from Africa who retained strong ties with African culture. In the case of the North Carolina revolt, the younger blacks—perhaps the first generation of American-born Negroes—proved the more pliant prisoners, whereas the older Negroes—possibly those born in Africa who maintained a strong sense of African identity—were recalcitrant and uncooperative. The slave Bob explained that the rebels were to divide up the lands among themselves. Declaring that "he would be no mans Slave," Moses upon seeing a certain white girl "had Repeatedly Said there goes my wife." Thomas Blount, in reporting the insurrection to his brother, explained that "when all the white men were killed the Black men were to take their places, have their wives &c. &c."[22]

For most white Carolinians the heritage of the Revolution had now taken on frightening ramifications. Decrying the scenes of "Blood and carnage" evident on "that unhappy Island where Black Touissant has the ruling power," Nathaniel Blount at the height of North Carolina's trauma attacked the "sticklers for liberty and equality (neither of which tho' in fact, they seem by any means to like to allow . . .)" and the "approvers of the principles and conduct of that Bloody minded people [Haiti's black revolutionists]."[23]

It would be easy, however, to overstate the insurgents' plans to replace their masters and claim white wives. Many clearly believed they were fighting "against the white people to obtain their liberty." Not a few of the conspirators associated the plot with a class revolt, for they anticipated reinforcements from "a number of poor people (white which they expected would Join Them)." And it is difficult to separate black intentions from white hysteria. By all accounts eastern North Carolina was in an uproar during the spring and summer of 1802. The militia in the counties were out in force, and "nearly every negro man was under guard." Various towns kept "a Strong guard Every Night." At least twenty-five blacks—a conservative figure—in North Carolina and Virginia were executed, sometimes "without giving them a legal Trial," and scores of others whipped and mutilated. One report stated that over one hundred Negroes were jailed in Martin County alone.

Throughout southern history deep apprehensions about Negro insurgencies have belied whites' self-confidence that blacks were docile. Such fears have most clearly manifested themselves in the insurrection panics of the antebellum era in which suspicions mushroomed into fantasies of black violence and retribution.[24] In such episodes the drama was played out in the imaginations of whites. But the insurrection scare was effective precisely because it was so widely believed. The phantom revolt became another means of social control, unifying southern whites, warning blacks against insubordination, and parrying the challenges of annoying dissenters like Quakers. Torture-induced confessions provided evidence when "facts" were missing.

The slave insurrection scare of 1802 in North Carolina unquestionably contained some of these elements. The political contests in the Old North State, as in the rest of the nation, had been hotly disputed by Federalists and Republicans. Slave unrest seemed epidemic. Quakers illegally manumitted slaves. The Great Revival, following on the heels of Baptist and Methodist proselytizing, encouraged blacks and whites to worship together and widened rifts within the white community.

Many of the slave confessions in 1802 were obtained through torture. Tight-lipped rebels would give "no information until whiped." A special committee of inquiry, formed to investigate the rumors, promised the younger slaves lenient treatment, and they readily confessed without the use of the lash. But the "old ones and chiefs amongst them, were true and faithful to their trust; not one of them would acknowledge at first that he knew anything of the plot. . . ." After being whipped, their confessions "agreed perfectly with the evidence of the others, that never received a stroke." The white investigators kept the compliant slaves in one jail and the militant ones in another. The former were then used as state witnesses against the ringleaders.[25]

Though white hysteria and excesses doubtless implicated a number of innocent blacks, the lesions of slave discontent burst forth in too many disparate parts of eastern North Carolina to have been the mere imaginings of anxious whites. Tom Copper in Pasquotank County and the rebels in Bertie, Martin, and Washington counties seem to have been the boldest and best organized. Indeed, the North Carolina insurrection shared certain features with other more famous slave plots. The North Carolina rebels, just as Gabriel Prosser in Richmond (1800), Denmark Vesey in Charleston (1822), and Nat Turner in Southampton County, Virginia (1831), included literate leaders who used those abilities to plan and execute the revolt. Each rebellion had an urban dimension: in the case of the North Carolina insurgents they were to rendezvous in Plymouth, and Tom Copper evidently delighted in harassing Elizabeth City. Prosser looked to the French for outside help, while the North Carolina blacks looked to Prosser and his Virginia revolutionists as well as poor whites to come to their aid. All the plots came in the wake of serious tensions within the white community: political divisions, religious awakenings, and debates on slavery. And each insurrection had its religious base. Prosser relied on Christian preaching; Vesey argued that the Bible sanctioned his revolt; Turner cast himself in the role of a black messiah; and the North Carolina blacks, who perhaps found their self-worth in evangelical Protestantism, most assuredly used the Great Revival and religion to advance their rebellion.[26]

The American South averted the massive slave revolts of the Caribbean in which thousands of slaves sometimes participated. The slave rebellions of colonial and antebellum North America rarely included more than one hundred slaves, and that appears to have been the case in North Carolina. Still for a few brief weeks in the spring and summer of 1802, the social, economic, and political trends of nearly 150 years were crystallized in North

Carolina. Though not as large nor as concentrated as slavery in Virginia and South Carolina, the institution in the Old North State was firmly entrenched. It had had small beginnings, despite the grandiose plans of the proprietors and Barbadians, and had not really begun to take root until the middle of the eighteenth century. The devastation of the Revolutionary War had briefly suspended the institution's growth, but by 1800 the slave population was expanding faster than ever.

With slavery's growth had come increasingly stringent laws and regulations for blacks. But through it all black Carolinians had struggled to maintain their human dignity, quietly but persistently had plotted out areas of autonomy for themselves, and when the occasion arose had gambled their lives for freedom by running away, fighting in the Revolution, or risking the perils of a slave revolt. Their legacy was no less revolutionary than the whites'. It remained to David Walker, who grew to maturity in the backwash of the Revolution, to articulate that legacy.

David Walker epitomized the Revolution's impact on Afro-Americans. Born in Wilmington, North Carolina, in 1785, Walker was a free black by virtue of his mother's status, though his father was a slave. While it is not known how he learned to read and write, Walker traveled widely through the United States and the South. Sometime in the 1820s he settled in Boston where he opened a shop near the wharves. Walker was a militant abolitionist who advocated servile insurrection, whatever the cost in blood, to overthrow the peculiar institution. In 1829 he penned *An Appeal to the Coloured Citizens of the World* which reverberated throughout the country and enraged the South. Quoting the Declaration of Independence directly in his fiery tract, Walker demanded: "Compare your own language . . . with your cruelties and murders inflicted by your cruel and unmerciful fathers and yourselves on our fathers and on us. . . . Now Americans! I ask you candidly, was your sufferings under Great Britain, one hundredth part as cruel and tyranical as you have rendered ours under you?"[27]

The South's furious answer was to suppress the inflammatory tome. A price was reportedly placed on Walker's head, and in 1830 he was found dead near the doorway of his shop. Poison was suspected. David Walker had dared to evince the view that the promise of the Revolution applied equally to all men. It would take a bloodier and costlier second American Revolution three decades later to resolve his vexing questions.

APPENDIX

The following list of North Carolina blacks who served in the Continental Line or the militia during the Revolutionary War has been compiled by the cooperative efforts of the author, George Stevenson of the State Archives, Lee Albright of the State Library, and Thomas Parramore of Meredith College. Most records do not identify soldiers by race, so that cross references have been made among censuses (especially those of 1790 and 1830), the Secretary of State Papers, and Revolutionary Pension Claims filed with the National Archives, as well as several other scattered sources. Especially helpful was the *Roster of Soldiers from North Carolina in the American Revolution*, privately printed by the Daughters of the American Revolution in 1932.

In 1783 the General Assembly authorized land warrants to Revolutionary War veterans; the size of the warrant depended on rank and years of service. The warrant entitled the veteran to have so many acres of land surveyed in present-day Tennessee. Having done that, the veteran could then claim a grant for the land. From the evidence it appears that few if any black veterans actually received a land grant. Most of those whom the legislature identified as eligible for land warrants had died in service, never claimed the warrants, or sold them to land speculators. Consequently, during the 1820s thousands of acres of land were escheated for the University of North Carolina. The history of these land warrants for Revolutionary veterans has yet to be written.

No claims are made for this list being definitive, but it does provide a corpus of evidence on the military service of black Carolinians.

JOSIAH ABSHIER   Abshier appeared in the 1830 census as a free Negro. According to an 1835 pension list, he was a former corporal receiving a pension worth $345.97.

JOSEPH ALLEN   Described as a mulatto planter; he mustered with the 6th Regiment on May 25, 1778, and later received a Revolutionary pension.

EVANS ARCHER   Listed as a free Negro in the 1790 census and a Revolutionary War pensioner in a report to Congress in 1835.

CHARLES BARNETT   Listed in 1830 as a free Negro in Granville County; he served in the Virginia militia and received a pension of $180 in 1831.

SAMUEL BELL   Listed as a free Negro in the 1790 census; he enlisted in the Continental Line in February, 1782, for twelve months. At the age of eighty-five in 1831 he received a pension of $109.98.

MOSES BIRD   A musician, described as a "man of colour," who enlisted in the 4th Regiment for three years on July 4, 1776. Said by one deponent to have died at Lancaster, Pa. Name omitted from roster in January, 1778, but another Moses Bird enlisted with the 10th Regiment on May 22, 1778, and mustered in January, 1779. Given a 274 acre land warrant in 1783; evidently never claimed, for the land (1,000 acres) escheated in 1821.

MARTIN BLACK   Listed in 1790 census as a free Negro; enlisted in May, 1777, in the 10th Regiment for three years; he reenlisted for eighteen months in 1782.

THOMAS BLANGO   Listed in 1790 census; served in the militia from the New Bern district.

DAVID BURNET   Described as a "man of colour," and a "war soldier in Blount's Company, and his waiter sometime." Enlisted April 2, 1776, for the war's duration in the 5th Regiment; omitted from the roster in February, 1778. Died without heirs and land warrant (640 acres) escheated, 1821.

CHARLES BURNETT   A mulatto, he enlisted for war's duration in 1780 with the 10th Regiment; said to have died with no heirs.

ISAAC CARTER   A mulatto, he enlisted with the 8th Regiment on September 1, 1777. According to one report he was killed in Pa. in 1778, but it appears more likely that he was taken prisoner on June 1, 1779, and discharged on February 20, 1780. For his three years' service, he received a land warrant in 1783 of 274 acres. Also listed as a free Negro in 1790 census.

DRURY CHAVIS   Described as "a Negro" who enlisted on May 25, 1781, for twelve months' service. According to one report, he was killed at the battle of Eutaw Springs, S.C., but he may have left the line on May 25, 1782. He died without heirs, and his land warrant (640 acres) was escheated, 1821.

JOHN CHAVIS   Famous Negro teacher of white and black students in Raleigh who served three years in the 5th

Virginia Regiment. He wrote Sen. Willie P. Mangum, one of his former students, in 1832, "Tell them that if I am Black I am free born American & a revolutionary soldier & therefore ought not to be thrown intirely out of the scale of notice."

CATO COPELAND   Listed in the 1790 census as a free Negro; enlisted for three years in 1776; a 1779 return for the 2nd Regiment shows him serving in same company as another Negro, Caesar Santee.

CUBIT   Described as a "free black man" who was a drummer; enlisted in 1777 in 1st Regiment for three-year stint; name omitted from roster in January, 1778. Believed to have died in a Wilmington, N.C., hospital; land warrant of 1,000 acres escheated in 1821.

RICHARD DAVIS   In a 1791 petition to the General Assembly Davis asserted that he had served as an artilleryman "in the cause of liberty. . . ." His wife had been emancipated by her master in 1784, and he had "enjoyed the Priviledges of a Freeman" since the war "without interruption." He asked that he and his children be legally emancipated.

JOHN DAY   Described as a "man of colour" from Granville County who enlisted on November 3, 1777, for the war's duration in the 2nd Regiment. Said to have died on January 14, 1778, after having served for two or three years. He may have committed suicide; "he died at Valley Forge . . . by taking a dose of physic and quickly afterwards drank freely of spirits which caused his death. . . ." In 1821 his brother Jesse Day sought to claim the land warrant due his brother.

JOHN ELLIS   Described as a "man of colour" who enlisted in 1776 and served until the end of the war. For seven years of service he was offered 640 acres in 1783. However, he never claimed the land and in 1821 sought another land warrant. He evidently conveyed a 228 acre warrant to Thomas Henderson at that time.

WILLIAM FOSTER   Described as a "man of colour" who enlisted in the 3d Regiment on June 15, 1779, for a term of eighteen months. He "was a regular soldier in the revolutionary army . . . and was taken prisoner at Charlestow[n], when the town was taken by the British."

FREDERICK   Described as a Negro musician in the 2nd Regiment; a drummer. Benjamin Robinson shared the same hut with him at Valley Forge, where the Negro died of a fever early in 1778.

BLACK GARRICK   A drummer who enlisted May 15, 1777, in the 4th Regiment for three years of duty. His name omitted from roster, January, 1778. A land warrant of 1,000 acres in his name escheated in 1821.

JENKENS GOWAN   Described as a mulatto; he mustered with the 6th Regiment on May 25, 1778.

NED GRIFFEN   A short time before the Battle of Guilford Court House William Kitchen deserted from the North Carolina Line but was returned to service. He thereupon purchased Ned Griffen, "a man of mixed blood," from William Griffen to serve as a substitute in the army and promised him his freedom for such service. Kitchen reneged on his promise, but the General Assembly granted Griffen his freedom in 1784; Griffen had served twelve months.

WILLIAM GUY   Listed in 1830 census as a free Negro from Granville County; he served in the Virginia Line and received a pension of $120 in 1831.

ISAAC HAMMOND   Described as a "man of colour" who enlisted November 1, 1781, in the 10th Regiment for twelve months. He was said to have died on James Island, S.C., on August 1, 1782, but his name appeared in 1790 census as a free Negro with a family of five.

WILLIAM HERSEY   According to a petition to the legislature in 1814, Hersey, a resident of Warren County, served in the Revolutionary War from July, 1782, until its conclusion. He did not appear on the muster roll "because he was detained as a waiter on General [Jethro] Sumner" while the latter recruited in N.C. Hersey described as a "man of colour."

CHARLES HOOD   In 1783 he received a land warrant of 274 acres, having served thirty-six months in the service. In the 1820s Hood gave important depositions on other blacks who had served. He ultimately received a pension.

DAVID IVEY   A "man of colour" and musician, he enlisted on May 12, 1777, in the 10th Regiment for a three-year term. In 1781 he was a waggoner. Granted a warrant of 274 acres in 1783; in 1820, however, his warrant, calculated at 154 acres, was given to the University of North Carolina.

FRANCIS JACK   Described as a "man of colour" who enlisted on June 19, 1779, for eighteen months of service in the 10th Regiment. He "marched to the South where he died"; name omitted from roster, October, 1779. No heirs; his 640 acre land warrant escheated, 1821.

BRUTUS JOHNSTON   Described as a "black man and private in the N.C. line, 10th Regt." A musician, he enlisted for three years on September 4, 1777; he died February 15, 1778. His 640 acre land warrant escheated in 1820s.

VALENTINE LOCUS   Enlisted in the 3d Regiment on April 22, 1776, for a term of thirty months; he received a 228 acre land warrant, and his wife Rachel applied for a Revolutionary pension in 1838; he had died in 1812.

JOB LOTT   He enlisted in 1777 for two and one-half years, but he died in June, 1777; served in 5th Regiment. According to Charles Hood, "Lott left no heirs South, he was a waggoner to the British army, came over to West Point & brought a load of flour which he sold to the Americans and enlisted in the service of the Continental Line."

BILLING LUCAS   Described as a "man of colour" who enlisted for nine months on June 5, 1779, in the 10th Regiment; he died September 5, 1779.

MOSES MANLEY   Listed in 1790 census as a free Negro; he enlisted for eighteen months in 1782 in the 10th Regiment. Also listed as a Revolutionary War pensioner in 1835.

ABSOLOM MARTIN   Listed in 1790 census as a free Negro; apparently received some back-pay for service in the Continentals during the 1780s.

MINGO   An armourer who enlisted in June, 1776, in North Carolina Line; name omitted from roster, September, 1777.

JONATHAN OVERTON   A newspaper account in 1849 described him as "a colored man, and a soldier of the Revolution, . . . at the advanced age of one hundred and one years. The deceased served under Washington, and was at the battle of Yorktown, besides other less important engagements."

ISAAC PERKINS   Listed in 1790 census as a free Negro; in May, 1777, he enlisted in the 10th Regiment for three years. In 1783 he was granted a land warrant of 274 acres for thirty-six months of service.

WILLIAM PETTIFORD   Described as a mulatto; he mustered with the 6th Regiment on May 25, 1778.

DEMPSEY REED   Listed in 1790 census as a free Negro; name also appeared in Revolutionary War accounts. Nathaniel Harris of Mecklenburg County hired him as a substitute; Reed was evidently wounded during the war.

JACK ROCK   Described as a "man of colour" and a "soldier and a Regular for the war in the Continental army." He enlisted June 18, 1779, for the war's duration in the 10th Regiment. His land warrant was escheated in 1821.

CAESAR SANTEE   Enlisted February 22, 1777, in the 2nd Regiment; taken prisoner June 1, 1779; mustered in 1781 for the war's duration. In 1783 he was given a land warrant of 640 acres for seven years' service.

HILL SCIPIO   Enlisted in the 10th Regiment in 1781 for twelve months; he left the service April 22, 1782.

LEWIS SIMMS   Described as a "black man" and planter who mustered with the 6th Regiment on May 25, 1778.

JAMES SMITH   Listed in 1790 census as a free Negro; in June, 1777, he enlisted in the 10th Regiment for three years; he reenlisted in December, 1781, for twelve more months; discharged in 1782. He may have been a waggoner.

JEREMIAH SMITH   According to a petition to Congress in 1851, Smith was the servant of John Smith of Johnston County and served in the Revolutionary War as a servant to officers in the army carrying expresses and performing other similar tasks. Congress turned down his bid for a pension.

WILLIAM TABURN, SR.   Listed in the state census of the 1780s as a free Negro; he served in the North Carolina militia and received a Revolutionary War pension of $103.92 in 1831.

POMPEY TERRY   Enlisted in 10th Regiment on August 1, 1782, for eighteen months; transferred in March, 1783.

JOHN TONEY   Enlisted in 1781 for twelve months in the 10th Regiment; said to have died of measles at James Island, S.C., April 1, 1781, but he appeared in the 1790 census as a free Negro with a family of five.

DRURY WALDEN   Listed in the 1790 census as a free Negro; a musician in the North Carolina militia; received a pension in 1813 at the age of seventy-two of $114.99.

JOHN WEAVER   Enlisted in July, 1777, for three years in 10th Regiment; in 1783 received a land warrant of 640 acres for seven years' service.

ARTHUR WIGGINS   Listed in 1830 census as free Negro; enlisted September, 1782, for eighteen months in the 10th Regiment. He received a Revolutionary War pension in 1835.

HENRY WIGGINS   Described as a "man of colour" who

enlisted April 11, 1777, for two and one-half years in the 3d Regiment; name omitted from roster, June, 1778. Said to have died on James Island, S.C. In 1821 his land warrant of 640 acres was escheated.

JOHN WOMBLE   Listed as free Negro in 1790 census; enlisted in June, 1779, for war's duration. He received a land warrant of 640 acres, based on seven years of service, in 1783; he served in the 10th Regiment.

NOTES

Chapter I

1. William L. Saunders (ed.), *The Colonial Records of North Carolina* (Raleigh, 10 vols., 1886-1890), III, 430, hereinafter cited as Saunders, *Colonial Records*.

2. Winthrop D. Jordan, *White Over Black: American Attitudes Toward the Negro, 1550-1812* (Chapel Hill, 1968), 44, hereinafter cited as Jordan, *White Over Black*.

3. Peter H. Wood, *Black Majority: Negroes in Colonial South Carolina from 1670 through the Stono Rebellion* (New York, 1974), 13-15, hereinafter cited as Wood, *Black Majority*.

4. Wood, *Black Majority*, 16.

5. Saunders, *Colonial Records*, I, 204.

6. William S. Powell (ed.), *Yᵉ Countie of Albemarle in Carolina: A Collection of Documents, 1664-1675* (Raleigh, 1958), 7.

7. Hugh T. Lefler and Albert R. Newsome, *North Carolina: The History of a Southern State* (Chapel Hill, Third Edition, 1973), 128-129.

8. Wood, *Black Majority*, Table I, p. 144; Table II, p. 146-147.

9. H. Roy Merrens, *Colonial North Carolina in the Eighteenth Century: A Study in Historical Geography* (Chapel Hill, 1964), 75, hereinafter cited as Merrens, *Colonial North Carolina*.

10. Merrens, *Colonial North Carolina*, 77-79.

11. Merrens, *Colonial North Carolina*, 123-133; Rosser H. Taylor, *Slaveholding in North Carolina: An Economic View* (Chapel Hill, 1926), 12-14, 19, hereinafter cited as Taylor, *Slaveholding in North Carolina*.

12. William S. Powell (ed.), "Tryon's 'Book' on North Carolina," *North Carolina Historical Review*, XXXIV (1957), 406-415, hereinafter cited as Powell, "Tryon's Book."

13. Marshall's Report, Aug. 3, 1770, Adelaide L. Fries and others (eds.), *Records of the Moravians in North Carolina* (Raleigh, 11 vols., 1922-1969), II, 614, hereinafter cited as Fries, *Moravian Records*.

14. Powell, "Tryon's Book," 411.

15. Powell, "Tryon's Book," 411.

16. John Urmston to the Society for the Propagation of the Gospel, July 7, 1711, Saunders, *Colonial Records*, I, 764.

17. Soelle's Diary, Sept. 20, 1772, Fries, *Moravian Records*, II, 780.

18. Johann David Schoepf, *Travels in the Confederation, 1783-1784*, ed. and trans. Alfred J. Morrison (Philadelphia, 2 vols., 1911), II, 117-118, hereinafter cited as Schoepf, *Travels in the Confederation*.

19. Charles Pettigrew to Nathaniel Allen, May 19, 1792 [1791], Sarah McCulloh Lemmon (ed.), *The Pettigrew Papers* (Raleigh, 1 vol. to date, 1971-), I, 103; Pettigrew to May L. Pettigrew, Oct. 1, 1795, I, 166-167; Pettigrew to Nathaniel Blount, [May, 1802], I, 285, hereinafter cited as Lemmon, *Pettigrew Papers*.

20. Eugene D. Genovese, *Roll, Jordan, Roll: The World the Slaves Made* (New York, 1974), 309-324, hereinafter cited as Genovese, *Roll, Jordan, Roll*.

21. Pettigrew to Rebecca Tunstall, June 22, 1803, Lemmon, *Pettigrew Papers*, I, 307.

22. Janet Schaw, *Journal of a Lady of Quality*, ed. Evangeline W. Andrews and Charles M. Andrews (New Haven, 1923), 194, hereinafter cited as Schaw, *Journal of a Lady of Quality*.

23. James M. Clifton, "Golden Grains of White: Rice Planting on the Lower Cape Fear," *North Carolina Historical Review*, L (1973), 365-369.

24. Wood, *Black Majority*, 58-60.

25. Wood, *Black Majority*, 61-62.

26. Schaw, *Journal of a Lady of Quality*, 163.

27. John Brickell, *The Natural History of North Carolina* (Dublin, 1737), 275-276, hereinafter cited as Brickell, *Natural History*.

28. Schoepf, *Travels in the Confederation*, II, 141.

29. Brickell, *Natural History*, 265-266; 33.

30. J. F. D. Smyth, *Tour in the United States of America* (London, 2 vols., 1784), I, 118-121, hereinafter cited as Smyth, *Tour of America*.

31. Brickell, *Natural History*, 275.

32. *North Carolina Gazette*, July 3, 1778.

33. British Records Collection, ADM 36/3902, North Carolina Division of Archives and History, Raleigh, hereinafter cited as British Records, State Archives.

34. William Blount to John Gray Blount, Aug. 11, 1787, Alice B. Keith and William H. Masterson (eds.), *The John Gray Blount Papers* (Raleigh, 3 vols. to date, 1952-), I, 335-336, hereinafter cited as *Blount Papers*.

35. Robert W. Fogel and Stanley L. Engerman, *Time on the Cross: The Economics of American Negro Slavery* (Boston, 1974). Herbert G. Gutman seriously challenges the methodology and conclusions of this work in his book, *Slavery and the Numbers Game: A Critique of* Time on the Cross (Urbana, Ill., 1975).

36. Alan D. Watson, "Society and Economy in Colonial Edgecombe County," *North Carolina Historical Review*, L (1973), 247-248.

37. Schoepf, *Travels in the Confederation*, II, 147.

38. Journals of Enos Reeves, Nov. 23, 1781, Manuscript Department, Duke University, hereinafter cited as Reeves Journal.

39. William Attmore, *Journal of a Tour to North Carolina by William Attmore, 1787*, ed. Lida T. Rodman (Chapel Hill, 1922), 38-39, 44, hereinafter cited as Attmore, *Tour to North Carolina*.

40. Hugh B. Johnston (ed.), "The Journal of Ebenezer Hazard in North Carolina, 1777 and 1778," *North Carolina Historical Review*, XXXVI (1959), 374, 377, hereinafter cited as Johnston, "Hazard Journal."

41. Smyth, *Tour of America*, I, 44-47.

42. Elkanah Watson, *Men and Times of the Revolution; or Memoirs of Elkanah Watson, including His Journals of Travels in Europe and America, 1777-1842*, ed. Winslow C. Watson (New York, Second Edition, 1857), 65-66, hereinafter cited as Watson, *Men and Times of the Revolution*.

43. Brickell, *Natural History*, 132, 137, 178, 200, 205.

44. Attmore, *Tour to North Carolina*, 26.

45. Schaw, *Journal of a Lady of Quality*, 176-177.

46. Scotus Americanus, "Informations Concerning the Province of North Carolina Etc. (1773)," in W. K. Boyd (ed.), *Some Eighteenth Century Tracts Concerning North Carolina* (Raleigh, 1927), 445-446; Brickell, *Natural History*, 275.

47. Walter Clark (ed.), *The State Records of North Carolina* (Winston and Goldsboro, 16 vols., 1895-1907), XXIII, 952, hereinafter cited as Clark, *State Records*.

48. Schoepf, *Travels in the Confederation*, II, 151.

49. Schaw, *Journal of a Lady of Quality*, 166, 176-177.

50. Smyth, *Tour of America*, I, 44-46.

51. Schaw, *Journal of a Lady of Quality*, 171.

52. Attmore, *Tour to North Carolina*, 17-18.

53. Brickell, *Natural History*, 274-275.
54. Herbert G. Gutman, *The Black Family in Slavery and Freedom, 1750-1925* (New York, 1976).
55. Burrington to Commissioners of Customs, July 20, 1736, Saunders, *Colonial Records*, IV, 172.
56. Watson, *Men and Times of the Revolution*, 69.
57. Schoepf, *Travels in the Confederation*, II, 148-149.
58. Schoepf, *Travels in the Confederation*, II, 148.
59. Watson, *Men and Times of the Revolution*, 69.

Chapter II

1. Saunders, *Colonial Records*, II, 197.
2. Saunders, *Colonial Records*, I, 639; II, 214-215.
3. Clark, *State Records*, XXIII, 63-65.
4. Brickell, *Natural History*, 168, 270, 272.
5. Brickell, *Natural History*, 272-273.
6. Clark, *State Records*, XXIII, 106-107.
7. Clark, *State Records*, XXIII, 194-203.
8. Brickell, *Natural History*, 276.
9. Clark, *State Records*, XXIII, 388-390.
10. Saunders, *Colonial Records*, III, 106; V, 1122.
11. Saunders, *Colonial Records*, IX, 398, 470, 663, 664.
12. Brickell, *Natural History*, 273.
13. Clark, *State Records*, XXIII, 488-489.
14. Marvin L. Michael Kay and Lorin Lee Cary, " 'The Planters Suffer Little or Nothing': North Carolina Compensations for Executed Slaves, 1748-1772," *Science and Society*, XI (Fall, 1976), 288-306.
15. John Spencer Bassett, *Slavery in the State of North Carolina* (Baltimore, 1899), 14, hereinafter cited as Bassett, *Slavery in North Carolina*.
16. Charles Pettigrew to Ebenezer Pettigrew, May 19, 1803, and Ebenezer Pettigrew to James Iredell, Jr., Dec. 31, 1806, Lemmon, *Pettigrew Papers*, I, 302-303; 398.
17. Donald R. Lennon and Ida B. Kellam (eds.), *The Wilmington Town Book, 1743-1778* (Raleigh, 1973), 18, hereinafter cited as *Wilmington Town Book*. Also see James H. Brewer, "Legislation Designed to Control Slavery in Wilmington and Fayetteville," *North Carolina Historical Review*, XXX (1953).
18. *Wilmington Town Book*, xxxi.
19. Fries, *Moravian Records*, II, 828.
20. *Wilmington Town Book*, 164-168.
21. *Wilmington Town Book*, 204-205.
22. *Wilmington Town Book*, 105, 125, 229, 237.
23. Clark, *State Records*, XXIV, 725-730.
24. Ira Berlin, *Slaves Without Masters: The Free Negro in the Antebellum South* (New York, 1975), 3-6, hereinafter cited as Berlin, *Slaves Without Masters*.
25. Saunders, *Colonial Records*, II, 672.
26. Jordan, *White Over Black*, 145.
27. Francisco de Miranda, *The New Democracy in America: Travels of Francisco de Miranda in the United States*, trans. Judson P. Wood, ed. John S. Ezell (Norman, Okla., 1963), 14.
28. Jordan, *White Over Black*, 145.
29. Johnston, "Hazard Journal," 376.
30. Clark, *State Records*, XXII, 370-372.

31. John Spencer Bassett, *Slavery and Servitude in the Colony of North Carolina* (Baltimore, 1896), 67.

32. Saunders, *Colonial Records*, V, 295; VI, 982-983; IX, 592.

33. Reeves Journal, Mar. 13, 1782.

34. John Hope Franklin, *The Free Negro in North Carolina, 1790-1860* (Chapel Hill, 1943), 106, hereinafter cited as Franklin, *Free Negro in North Carolina*.

35. Saunders, *Colonial Records*, IX, 803-804.

36. Saunders, *Colonial Records*, II, 555, 557.

37. Case of John Scott, 1767-1770, Treasurer's and Comptroller's Papers, Misc., Slaves, 1738-1863, State Archives.

38. Franklin, *Free Negro in North Carolina*, 54.

39. *North Carolina Gazette*, April 10, 1778.

40. Perquimans County Slave Papers, 1759-1799, State Archives.

41. Slavery Papers, Miscellaneous Collection, State Archives, hereinafter cited as Slavery Papers, Misc., State Archives.

Chapter III

1. Saunders, *Colonial Records*, II, 327.

2. Saunders, *Colonial Records*, IV, 922.

3. Jean Blair to Hannah Iredell, May 24, 1781; Blair to James Iredell, June 5, 1781; Blair to Hannah Iredell, Oct. 7, 1781, Don Higginbotham (ed.), *The Papers of James Iredell* (Raleigh, 2 vols. to date, 1976), II, 246, 255, 309, hereinafter cited as Higginbotham, *Iredell Papers*.

4. Blair to Hannah Iredell, May 24, 1781, Higginbotham, *Iredell Papers*, II 246-247. Charles Pettigrew, writing in 1797, offered this trenchant advice to his sons: "To manage *negroes* without the exercise of too much passion, is next to an impossibility. . . . I would therefore put you on your guard, lest their provocations should on some occasions transport you beyond the limits of decency and christian morality." There was no reason for slaves to be industrious, Pettigrew said, when they were bound for life and not laboring for themselves. Quoted in Guion G. Johnson, *Ante-Bellum North Carolina* (Chapel Hill, 1937), 496, hereinafter cited as Johnson, *Ante-Bellum North Carolina*.

5. Mattie Erma Edwards Parker and others (eds.), *The Colonial Records of North Carolina, Second Series* (Raleigh, 5 vols. to date, 1963-), II, 364; hereinafter cited as Parker, *Colonial Records, Second Series*.

6. Saunders, *Colonial Records*, VII, 685-686.

7. Thomas B. Haughton to Ebenezer Pettigrew, Aug. 15, 1803, Lemmon, *Pettigrew Papers*, I, 313.

8. Trial of Negro Sam, April 18, 1793, Bertie County Slave Papers, State Archives.

9. Slavery Papers, Misc., State Archives.

10. Wood, *Black Majority*, 289; John W. Blassingame, *The Slave Community: Plantation Life in the Antebellum South* (New York, 1972), 32-33, 45-48, hereinafter cited as Blassingame, *Slave Community*.

11. Trial of Slave Bristoe, Oct. 16, 1779, Johnston County Papers, Special Court for Trials of Negroes, 1764-1780, State Archives.

12. Trial of Jenny, Nov. 8, 1780, Johnston County Papers, Special Court for Trials of Negroes, State Archives.

13. Deposition of Sarah Wiggens, April 12, 1772, Slavery Papers, Misc., State Archives.

14. Saunders, *Colonial Records*, I, 654.

15. Trial of Peter, Aug. 17, 1785, Slavery Papers, Misc., State Archives.

16. *Virginia Gazette* (Purdie), Sept. 6, 1770.

17. Trial of Sam, Mar. 16, 1786, Slavery Papers, Misc., State Archives.

18. Granville County Papers, Criminal Action concerning Slaves and Free Negroes, 1762-1859, document dated April 26, 1783, State Archives.

19. Clark, *State Records*, XIX, 258.

20. Alexander M. Walker (ed.), *New Hanover County Court Minutes* (Bethesda, Md., 4 vols., 1958-1960), I, 40, hereinafter cited as Walker, *New Hanover Court Minutes*.

21. Parker, *Colonial Records, Second Series*, III, 241, 514.

22. Gerald W. Mullin, *Flight and Rebellion: Slave Resistance in Eighteenth-Century Virginia* (New York, 1972), 110-111, hereinafter cited as Mullin, *Flight and Rebellion*.

23. Willie Lee Rose (ed.), *A Documentary History of Slavery in North America* (New York, 1976), 57-58, hereinafter cited as Rose, *Documentary History*.

24. Mullin, *Flight and Rebellion*, 112.

25. Smyth, *Tour of America*, I, 101-102.

26. Watson, *Men and Times of the Revolution*, 51-52.

27. Walker, *New Hanover Court Minutes*, I, 80.

28. Wood, *Black Majority*, 240-241.

29. Jacob Blount to J. G. Blount, May 18, 1789, *Blount Papers*, I, 480.

30. Micaj Thomas to Thomas Blount, Aug. 31, 1783, *Blount Papers*, I, 99.

31. John Wallace to J. G. Blount, July 17, 1793, *Blount Papers*, II, 288.

32. *North Carolina Gazette*, May 5, 1775.

33. *North Carolina Gazette*, Nov. 21, 1777.

34. *North Carolina Gazette*, Feb. 24, 1775.

35. Andrew Miller to Thomas Burke, Feb. 22, 1774, Saunders, *Colonial Records*, IX, 826-827.

36. *Virginia Gazette*, Nov. 5, 1767, as quoted in Rose, *Documentary History*, 57.

37. *North Carolina Gazette*, Aug. 8, 1777.

38. *North Carolina Gazette*, Mar. 13, 1778.

39. Brickell, *Natural History*, 263, 357; Thomas Iredell to James Iredell, June 20, 1769, Higginbotham, *Iredell Papers*, I, 29-30.

40. Report on the Survey of the North Carolina-South Carolina Boundary, 1769, Clark, *State Records*, XI, 226-227.

41. Wood, *Black Majority*, 263.

42. Walker, *New Hanover Court Minutes*, I, 69.

43. Bassett, *Slavery in North Carolina*, 46, 56.

44. Saunders, *Colonial Records*, III, 112.

45. Blassingame, *Slave Community*, 61-63.

46. Saunders, *Colonial Records*, VII, 705.

47. C. E. Taylor to S.P.G., Aug. 24, 1772, Saunders, *Colonial Records*, IX, 326.

48. Alexander Stewart to S.P.G., Nov. 6, 1763, Saunders, *Colonial Records*, VI, 995-996; Alice E. Mathews, *Society in Revolutionary North Carolina* (Raleigh, 1976), 65-66.

49. James Reed to S.P.G., June 26, 1760, Saunders, *Colonial Records*, VI, 265.

50. "Autobiography of Omar ibn Seid in North Carolina, 1831," *American Historical Review*, XXX (1925), 791-795.

51. Blassingame, *Slave Community*, 64.

52. Edward Warren, *A Doctor's Experiences in Three Continents* (Baltimore, 1885), as quoted in William S. Tarlton, *Somerset Place and Its Restoration* (Raleigh, 1954), 82-85. According to the *Oxford English Dictionary*, Bairam is the name of two Mohammedan festivals—the lesser lasting

three days, and the greater, seventy days later, lasting four days.

53. Bassett, *Slavery in North Carolina*, 92-93.

54. Jerry L. Surratt, "The Role of Dissent in Community Evolution among Moravians in Salem, 1772-1860," *North Carolina Historical Review*, LII (1975), 249-250.

55. For a provocative discussion of some of these themes, see Rhys Isaac, "Evangelical Revolt: The Nature of the Baptists' Challenge to the Traditional Order in Virginia, 1765-1775," *William and Mary Quarterly*, 3d ser., XXI (1974).

56. Donald G. Mathews, *Slavery and Methodism: A Chapter in American Morality, 1780-1845* (Princeton, 1965), 3-29; Larry E. Tise, "North Carolina Methodism from the Revolution to the War of 1812" in *Methodism Alive in North Carolina*, ed. O. Kelly Ingram (Durham, 1976), 35, 44-46; Johnson, *Ante-Bellum North Carolina*, 545.

57. Saunders, *Colonial Records*, VII, 164.

58. *Virginia Gazette* (Purdie), June 13, 1777; May 1, 1778.

59. W. Harrison Daniel, "Virginia Baptists and the Negro in the Early Republic," *Virginia Magazine of History and Biography*, LXXX (1972), 60-62, hereinafter cited as Daniel, "Virginia Baptists."

60. Henry S. Stroupe, " 'Cite Them Both to Attend the Next Church Conference': Social Control by North Carolina Baptist Churches, 1772-1908," *North Carolina Historical Review*, LII (1975), 158-159.

61. Joseph Biggs, *A Concise History of the Kehukee Baptist Association* . . . (Tarborough, 1834), 47-48, 60, hereinafter cited as Biggs's *History of Kehukee Baptist Association*.

62. George W. Purefoy, *A History of the Sandy Creek Baptist Association* . . . (New York, 1859), 76, 84; Daniel, "Virginia Baptists," 65.

63. Lemuel Burkitt and Jesse Read, *Concise History of the Kehukee Baptist Association* . . . (Halifax, 1803), 77-78, hereinafter cited as Burkitt's *History of the Kehukee Baptist Association*.

64. Daniel, "Virginia Baptists," 62.

65. Burkitt's *History of the Kehukee Baptist Association*, 258-260.

66. Daniel, "Virginia Baptists," 60.

67. Biggs's *History of Kehukee Baptist Association*, 95-96.

68. Blassingame, *Slave Community*, 66, 71.

Chapter IV

1. Thomas C. Barrow, "The American Revolution as a Colonial War of Independence," *William and Mary Quarterly*, 3d ser., XXV (1968), 452-464.

2. The classic study of blacks in the Revolution remains Benjamin Quarles, *The Negro in the American Revolution* (Chapel Hill, 1961), hereinafter cited as Quarles, *The Negro in the Revolution*. In recent years several historians have begun to ask new questions about the black experience in the Revolution. Two excellent essays are James W. St. G. Walker, "Blacks as American Loyalists: The Slaves' War for Independence," *Historical Reflections*, II (Summer, 1975), 51-67, hereinafter cited as Walker, "Blacks as American Loyalists"; and Peter H. Wood, " 'Taking Care of Business' in Revolutionary South Carolina: Republicanism and the Slave Society," in *The Southern Experience in the American Revolution*, ed. Jeffrey J. Crow and Larry E. Tise (Chapel Hill: University of North Carolina Press, 1978).

3. Hugh F. Rankin, *The North Carolina Continentals* (Chapel Hill, 1971), 29.

4. Joseph Hewes to Samuel Johnston, July 8, 1775, Saunders, *Colonial*

Records, X, 86; Hewes to James Iredell, July 8, 1775, Higginbotham, *Iredell Papers*, I, 313.

5. Higginbotham, *Iredell Papers*, I, 409.

6. Saunders, *Colonial Records*, IX, 1046.

7. Leora H. McEachern and Isabel M. Williams (eds.), *Wilmington-New Hanover Safety Committee Minutes, 1774-1776* (Wilmington, 1974), 5, 20, hereinafter cited as *Safety Committee Minutes*. The committee, of course, may also have been deferring to Harnett, the Lower Cape Fear's most prominent rebel.

8. Saunders, *Colonial Records*, X, 72; *Safety Committee Minutes*, 30, 43.

9. *Safety Committee Minutes*, 45, 47.

10. Schaw, *Journal of a Lady of Quality*, 199.

11. Schaw, *Journal of a Lady of Quality*, 199-200.

12. Schaw, *Journal of a Lady of Quality*, 200-201. John Stuart, the crown's southern Indian agent, also discounted as so much propaganda rumors of a slave revolt. Stuart to the Earl of Dartmouth, July 21, 1775, Saunders, *Colonial Records*, X, 118.

13. Quarles, *The Negro in the Revolution*, 21n.

14. Martin to DeRossett, June 24, 1775, Saunders, *Colonial Records*, X, 138; *Virginia Gazette* (Pinkney), Aug. 31, 1775.

15. Saunders, *Colonial Records*, X, 87.

16. John Simpson to Richard Cogdell, July 15, 1775, Richard Cogdell Papers, State Archives; the same letter appears in Saunders, *Colonial Records*, X, 94-95.

17. See, for instance, Sir Peter Parker's use of "negro pilot Sampson" at assault on Charlestown, *Virginia Gazette* (Purdie), July 12, 1776; and on the importance of pilots to military operations, Capt. Gayton to Vice Admiral Arbuthnot, Oct. 20, 1780, English Records, ADM 1/486, 1015-1026, State Archives.

18. Quarles, *The Negro in the Revolution*, 19.

19. *Virginia Gazette* (Purdie), Nov. 17, 1775.

20. *Virginia Gazette* (Dixon and Hunter), Dec. 2, 1775.

21. *Virginia Gazette* (Purdie), Jan. 19, 1776.

22. *North Carolina Gazette*, Dec. 22, 1775.

23. *Virginia Gazette* (Purdie), May 24, 1776.

24. Saunders, *Colonial Records*, X, 567, 569.

25. Saunders, *Colonial Records*, IX, 1026.

26. Peter Kent Opper, "North Carolina Quakers: Reluctant Slaveholders," *North Carolina Historical Review*, LII (1975), 37-38. A number of Quaker documents related to antislavery convictions are conveniently printed in Robert M. Calhoon, *Religion and the American Revolution in North Carolina* (Raleigh, 1976), 41-49, hereinafter cited as Calhoon, *Religion in North Carolina*.

27. Clark, *State Records*, XXIV, 14-15.

28. Johnston, "Hazard Journal," 362-363.

29. Clark, *State Records*, XXIV, 221.

30. Clark, *State Records*, XIII, 659-660.

31. Opper, "North Carolina Quakers," 38.

Chapter V

1. Pete Maslowski, "National Policy toward the Use of Black Troops in the Revolution," *South Carolina Historical Magazine*, LXXIII (1972); Berlin, *Slaves Without Masters*, 18-19.

2. See the letters exchanged between Nathanael Greene and Gov. Martin of Georgia, dated Feb. 2, Mar. 15, and June 8, 1782, in the Nathanael Greene Papers, Duke University, hereinafter cited as Greene Papers.

3. Jacob Turner's Diary, Clark, *State Records*, XII, 539.

4. Alexander Scammell, Return of Negro Troops, Aug. 24, 1778, George Washington Papers, Library of Congress.

5. Petition by Ned Griffin, Mar. 27, 1784, Legislative Papers, 50, State Archives; Clark, *State Records*, XXIV, 639.

6. General Gates's Orders, Aug. 15, 1780, English Records, CO 5/183/163, State Archives.

7. See Appendix. The sources for this list of blacks who served in the North Carolina Line or militia are too numerous to cite. The information has been culled from cross references to state and federal censuses, especially the ones in 1790 and 1830, and such sources as the Secretary of State, Revolutionary Military Papers, State Archives; Revolutionary War Pension and Bounty-Land-Warrant Application Files, National Archives; and a roster of Continental soldiers from North Carolina, compiled by the Daughters of the American Revolution, and available in the State Archives.

8. Pension Claim for Isaac Hammond, W 7654, National Archives.

9. *North Carolina Gazette*, Sept. 26, 1777.

10. Petition by Thomas Newby for slave James, n.d., Perquimans County Slave Papers, Petitions for Emancipation, 1776-1825, State Archives.

11. Hugh McDonald's Diary, Clark, *State Records*, XI, 834.

12. Pension Claim for John Toney, W 9859, National Archives.

13. Diary of the Congregation in Salem, Feb. 4, 1781, Fries, *Moravian Records*, IV, 1672.

14. Orange County Court Minutes, 1777-1788, Part I, Dec. 19 and 23, 1780, State Archives.

15. Clark, *State Records*, XXIV, 350-351.

16. *North Carolina Gazette*, Sept. 12, 1777.

17. Clark, *State Records*, XII, 150.

18. Robert Burton Papers, voucher dated Sept. 19, 1782, Duke University.

19. Clark, *State Records*, XX, 57.

20. J. Burnet to Andrew Pickens, June 7, 1781; Greene to Joseph Clay, June 9, 1781, Greene Papers.

21. Clark, *State Records*, XV, 197-198; XXIV, 338, 491, 954.

22. Don Higginbotham, *The War of American Independence: Military Attitudes, Policies, and Practice, 1763-1789* (New York, 1971), 396.

23. Clark, *State Records*, XI, 708.

24. Quarles, *The Negro in the Revolution*, 113.

25. "List of the Names of the Negroes belonging to Capt. Martin's Company, who they belonged to and the respective places they lived at," copy from the Sir Henry Clinton Papers, Clements Library, University of Michigan, held by the State Archives.

26. Loyalist Claim by Isaac DuBois, 1789, British Records, AO 12/73, State Archives.

27. Loyalist Claim by John Provey, 1784, British Records, AO 13/123, State Archives.

28. British Records, ADM 36/8377, State Archives.

29. British Records, ADM 36/8434, State Archives.

30. Walker, "Blacks as American Loyalists," 54.

31. See Ronald B. Hoffman, "The 'Disaffected' in the Revolutionary South," in *The American Revolution: Explorations in the History of American Radicalism*, ed. Alfred Young (DeKalb, Ill., 1976), 273-316.

32. Greene to Pickens, June 5, 1781, Greene Papers.

33. Letter to Alexander Martin, Dec. 19, 1781, Clark, *State Records*, XXII, 602-603.

34. Clark, *State Records*, XIV, 2-3; 308.

35. Charles Stedman, *History of the American War* (London, 2 vols., 1794), II, 217n.

36. Clinton to Cornwallis, May 20, 1780, Cornwallis Papers, PRO 30/11/2, folio 38-39, Library of Congress.

37. Balfour to Cornwallis, June 24, 1780, Cornwallis Papers, PRO 30/11/2, folio 191-196, Library of Congress.

38. Cornwallis to James Weymss, Aug. 31, 1780, Cornwallis Papers, PRO 30/11/79, folio 54, Library of Congress.

39. Balfour to Cruden, Aug. 22, 1781, Cornwallis Papers, PRO 30/11/30, Library of Congress.

40. *Royal Gazette* (Charlestown), Mar. 14, 1781, contains lists of the names of Negroes and their owners in the various departments.

41. Stedman, *History of the American War*, II, 354-355n.

42. Albert R. Newsome (ed.), "A British Orderly Book, 1780-1781," *North Carolina Historical Review*, IX (1932), 370, hereinafter cited as Newsome, "British Orderly Book."

43. Newsome, "British Orderly Book," 276, 280, 287.

44. Newsome, "British Orderly Book," 296-297.

45. Murfree to Nash, Nov. 1, 1780, Clark, *State Records*, XV, 138.

46. Turnbull to Lord Rawdon, Oct. 23, 1780, Cornwallis Papers, PRO 30/11/3, folio 263-264, Library of Congress.

47. Jean Blair to Helen Blair, Jan. 4, 1781; Blair to Hannah Iredell, May 10, 19, June 5, 1781, Higginbotham, *Iredell Papers*, II, 203, 239, 245, 257.

48. Blair to James Iredell, July 21, 1781, Higginbotham, *Iredell Papers*, II, 266.

49. Loyalist Claim by Samuel Marshall, 1789, British Records, AO 12/74, State Archives; Nathan Bryan to Gov. Burke, Sept. 6, 1781, Clark, *State Records*, XV, 634-635; William Caswell to Gov. Burke, Sept. 4, 1781, Clark, *State Records*, XXII, 593.

50. William Hooper to James Iredell, Feb. 17, 1782, Higginbotham, *Iredell Papers*, II, 329.

51. Cornwallis to Gen. O'Hara, Aug. 4, 1781, Charles Ross (ed.), *Correspondence of Charles, First Marquis Cornwallis* (London, 3 vols., 1859), I, 112; Benedict Arnold to _____, Feb. 13, 1781, English Records, CO 5/8, State Archives; Cornwallis to Gov. Thomas Nelson, Aug. 6, 1781, Cornwallis Papers, PRO 30/11/90, folio 19-20, Library of Congress.

52. *Royal Gazette* (Charlestown), Mar. 3, 1781.

53. Blair to James Iredell, July 21, 1781, Higginbotham, *Iredell Papers*, II, 266-267.

54. Quarles, *The Negro in the Revolution*, 149.

55. Return of Provincial Troops, Mar. 8, 1780, English Records, CO 5/8, State Archives; John Holloway to Messrs. Curson and Gouverneur, Nov. 25, 1780, English Records, CO 5/307, State Archives; Account of stoppages due from North Carolina militia to His Majesty's Hospital at Wilmington, Oct. 25-Nov. 25, 1781, English Records, T 50/5; Return of refugees from North Carolina, Charlestown, Dec. 1, 1781, Loyalist Militia, English Records, T 50/5; Clark, *State Records*, XVI, 155; James Iredell to Joseph Hewes, April 29, 1776, Higginbotham, *Iredell Papers*, I, 356.

56. Muster roll of Capt. William Darby's company of the Jamaica Corps, Feb. 24, 1781, English Records, SP 41/29; Recruiting list of Continental prisoners who enlisted in British army for service in West Indies, Feb. 9, 1782, English Records, SP 41/29, State Archives.

57. Leslie to Clinton, Mar. 12, 1782, Mar. 30, 1782, Mar., 1782, *Report of American Manuscripts in the Royal Institutions of Great Britain* (London and Dublin, 4 vols., 1904-1909), II, 417, 435, 438, hereinafter cited as *Report of American Manuscripts;* Walker, "Blacks as American Loyalists," 58-59.

58. Balfour to Cornwallis, Sept. 22, 1780, Cornwallis Papers, PRO 30/11/64, folio 96-97, Library of Congress.

59. Leslie to Carleton, Oct. 18, 1782, *Report of American Manuscripts*, III, 175-176.

60. James Moncrief to Henry Clinton, Mar. 13, 1782, *Report of American Manuscripts*, II, 419; Leslie to Carleton, June 27, 1782; Oct. 3, 1782, *Report of American Manuscripts*, II, 544; III, 150.

61. Gov. John Mathews to Gen. Leslie, Oct. 12, 1782, Secretary of State, Misc. In-Letters, PRO 448, CO 5/307, folio 223, Library of Congress; Sylvia R. Frey, "The British and the Black: A New Perspective," *The Historian*, XXXVIII (1976); Walker, "Blacks as American Loyalists," 62; James Iredell to Hannah Iredell, Nov. 20, 1782, Higginbotham, *Iredell Papers*, II, 361-362.

62. Quarles, *The Negro in the Revolution*, 168-172; Walker, "Blacks as American Loyalists," 62-64.

63. Walker, "Blacks as American Loyalists," 64n.

64. J. Leitch Wright, Jr., "Blacks in British East Florida," *Florida Historical Quarterly*, LIV (1976).

Chapter VI

1. Carole W. Troxler, *The Loyalist Experience in North Carolina* (Raleigh, 1976), 49-54; Walker, "Blacks as American Loyalists," 65-66.

2. Clark, *State Records*, XVII, 385, 389, 595-596; XVIII, 571-572, 623-625, 662-663, 680-681.

3. Case of Harry, Dinah, and Patt, April 5, 1785, Perquimans County Slave Papers; Account of sales of Negroes, 1788, Perquimans County Slave Papers; Case of Negro Judy, n.d., Perquimans County Slave Papers, 1759-1799, State Archives.

4. Clark, *State Records*, XXI, 762-763, 1004, 1019-1020.

5. Grand Jury Presentment, December, 1795, Pasquotank County Slave Papers, State Archives.

6. Jordan, *White Over Black*, 327.

7. Grand Jury Presentment, December, 1795, Pasquotank County Slave Papers, State Archives.

8. Herbert Aptheker, *American Negro Slave Revolts* (New York, 1943), 213, hereinafter cited as Aptheker, *American Negro Slave Revolts*.

9. Johnson, *Ante-Bellum North Carolina*, 551; Clark, *State Records*, XXIV, 890-891.

10. Aptheker, *American Negro Slave Revolts*, 217.

11. P. Manyeon to Benjamin Smith, Dec. 2, 1795, Slavery Papers, Misc., State Archives.

12. Taylor, *Slaveholding in North Carolina*, 25.

13. Trial of three Negro men, May 31, 1798, Bertie County Slave Papers, State Archives.

14. Trial of Quillo, April, 1794, Granville County Papers, State Archives.

15. *Raleigh Register*, June 1, 1802; Aptheker, *American Negro Slave Revolts*, 231-232.

16. William Henry Foote, *Sketches of North Carolina, Historical and Biographical . . .* (New York, 1846), 392, 402-403.

17. The sources for this plot are too numerous to cite for each individual quotation. The information, unless specified, has been culled from the Slavery Papers, Misc.; Perquimans County Slave Papers, 1759-1864; Bertie County Slave Papers, 1801-1805, State Archives; and *Raleigh Register*, May-July, 1802.

18. Trial of Dr. Joe, May 22, 1802, Pasquotank County Court Minutes, 1799-1802; Calhoon, *Religion in North Carolina*, 66-68.

19. See the correspondence between William R. Davie and Gov. Williams, February, 1802, in the Governor's Letterbook (Benjamin Williams), pp. 542, 552, 556, 560, 565, State Archives.

20. *Raleigh Register*, July 6, 1802.

21. *Raleigh Register*, June 22, July 27, 1802; Charles Pettigrew to Ebenezer Pettigrew, June 21, 1802, Lemmon, *Pettigrew Papers*, I, 287-288.

22. Thomas Blount to J. G. Blount, June 28, 1802, *Blount Papers*, III, 516-517. My thinking on this subject has been influenced to a considerable extent by Michael Mullin's provocative essay, "British Caribbean and North American Slaves in an Era of War and Revolution, 1775-1807," in Crow and Tise, *Southern Experience in Revolution*.

23. Nathaniel Blount to Charles Pettigrew, May 4, 1802, Lemmon, *Pettigrew Papers*, I, 283.

24. For a cogent discussion of this phenomenon, see Dan T. Carter, "The Anatomy of Fear: The Christmas Day Insurrection Scare of 1865," *Journal of Southern History*, XLII (1976), 345-364.

25. *Raleigh Register*, July 27, 1802.

26. On slave revolts, see Genovese, *Roll, Jordan, Roll*, 587-597.

27. David Walker, *David Walker's Appeal in Four Articles; Together with a Preamble to the Coloured Citizens of the World, But in Particular, and Very Expressly, To Those of the United States of America*, 3d edition, ed. Charles M. Wiltse (New York, 1965), 74-75.

BIBLIOGRAPHICAL ESSAY

The study of Afro-Americans in North Carolina must begin with secondary sources which have become more dated with each passing decade. While university and commercial publishing houses have poured forth a plethora of new works on slavery in the past decade, relatively few of them have focused directly on North Carolina, and none has undertaken the analysis of the peculiar institution in this state alone. The seminal studies of slavery in North Carolina were written by John Spencer Bassett in the 1890s: *Slavery and Servitude in the Colony of North Carolina* (Baltimore, 1896), and *Slavery in the State of North Carolina* (Baltimore, 1899). Though these books overlap, they still contain much useful material. Rosser H. Taylor's *Slaveholding in North Carolina: An Economic View* (Chapel Hill, 1926) has been superseded for the most part by relevant sections of H. Roy Merrens's invaluable *Colonial North Carolina in the Eighteenth Century: A Study in Historical Geography* (Chapel Hill, 1964). The most comprehensive study of slavery in North Carolina remains the pertinent chapters in Guion G. Johnson's *Ante-Bellum North Carolina* (Chapel Hill, 1937). Also suggestive is Edward W. Phifer's prize-winning article, "Slavery in Microcosm: Burke County, North Carolina," in the *Journal of Southern History*, XXVIII (1962).

The problem with most of the aforementioned works is that they concentrate on the antebellum period, ignoring the evolution of slavery in the colonial and Revolutionary period. Recent work by Marvin L. Michael Kay and Lorin Lee Cary, notably " 'The Planters Suffer Little or Nothing': North Carolina Compensations for Executed Slaves, 1748-1772," *Science and Society*, XI (1976), promises to begin reversing this imbalance.

Of the numerous new books on slavery, this study has profited most from Peter H. Wood's *Black Majority: Negroes in Colonial South Carolina from 1670 through the Stono Rebellion* (New York, 1974). Wood has advanced the understanding of slavery in the colonial period immeasurably with this highly original and insightful book. Eugene D. Genovese's *Roll, Jordan, Roll: The World the Slaves Made* (New York, 1974) provides a broad analysis of many aspects of antebellum slavery, and his Marxist approach brings a provocative perspective to the subject. Winthrop D. Jordan's *White Over Black: American Attitudes*

Toward the Negro, 1550-1812 (Chapel Hill, 1968) is unsurpassed in its coverage of slavery's growth in America before the nineteenth century. Also useful is Gerald W. Mullin's *Flight and Rebellion: Slave Resistance in Eighteenth-Century Virginia* (New York, 1972) which should be compared with Edmund S. Morgan's *American Slavery—American Freedom: The Ordeal of Colonial Virginia* (New York, 1975), a study that emphasizes political economy rather than race in explaining slavery's inception. The best treatment of the infrastructure of black life is John W. Blassingame's *The Slave Community: Plantation Life in the Antebellum South* (New York, 1972), and Willie Lee Rose's edited work, *A Documentary History of Slavery in North America* (New York, 1976), should preclude the need for another such study for years to come.

On free blacks North Carolina historians are fortunate to have the wisdom of John Hope Franklin in his pioneering study, *The Free Negro in North Carolina, 1790-1860* (Chapel Hill, 1943). Ira Berlin's important new work, *Slaves Without Masters: The Free Negro in the Antebellum South* (New York, 1975), gives a comprehensive analysis of the subject and provides revealing comparisons between the Upper South and Lower South.

Primary sources on slavery in North Carolina are sparse. Students of this state's history, however, will be eternally indebted to the monumental works of William L. Saunders and Walter Clark, *The Colonial Records of North Carolina* (Raleigh, 10 vols., 1886-1890) and *The State Records of North Carolina* (Winston and Goldsboro, 16 vols., 1895-1907), respectively. *The Colonial Records of North Carolina, Second Series* (Raleigh, 5 vols. to date, 1963-) under the editorship of Mattie E. E. Parker and others promises to produce much more information on the status of Negroes in the colonial period. Of the documentaries published by the North Carolina Division of Archives and History, researchers will find exceptional material on blacks in *The Pettigrew Papers* (Raleigh, 1 vol. to date, 1971-), edited by Sarah M. Lemmon; *The Wilmington Town Book, 1743-1778* (Raleigh, 1973), edited by Donald R. Lennon and Ida B. Kellam; and particularly *The Papers of James Iredell* (Raleigh, 2 vols. to date, 1976-), edited by Don Higginbotham.

The North Carolina State Archives in Raleigh hold some excellent manuscript sources which compensate for the relative dearth of private papers—compared to the antebellum period—that normally provide insights into blacks and slavery. The records of numerous counties contain essential data on blacks. The British Records, copied or microfilmed in London for the Colonial Records Project, remain an untapped mother lode of information. The collection of Nathanael Greene Papers at Duke University offers little on North Carolina itself during the Revolution, but it crackles with the gunfire of the late stages of the southern campaign.

Travelers' accounts are indispensable for an understanding of eighteenth-century North Carolina. Janet Schaw's *Journal of a Lady of Quality* (New Haven, 1923), edited by Evangeline W. Andrews and Charles M. Andrews, is especially good for the opening maneuvers of the patriots in the Revolution. Over the years John Brickell has been maligned as a plagiarist of John Lawson's earlier work, but Brickell's *The Natural History of North Carolina* (Dublin, 1737) offers an unparalleled description of Negroes in the colonial period. Other contemporary accounts that may be used with profit include William Attmore, *Journal of a Tour to North Carolina by William Attmore, 1787* (Chapel Hill, 1922), edited by Lida T. Rodman; and Johann David Schoepf, *Travels in the Confederation, 1783-1784* (Philadelphia, 2 vols., 1911), edited and translated by Alfred J. Morrison.

North Carolina newspapers were published haphazardly from the 1750s until the 1790s, but among others the *North Carolina Gazette*, published in New Bern by James Davis, remains a valuable source. Historians of North Carolina have sometimes neglected the newspapers of Virginia and South Carolina. The *Virginia Gazette*, actually several discrete papers with different editors, yields significant information on North Carolina. Loyalist newspapers published in Charlestown during the Revolutionary War contain accounts of people and activities in North Carolina, especially the *Royal Gazette*.

On the Revolution itself the classic study of Afro-Americans is still Benjamin Quarles, *The Negro in the American Revolution* (Chapel Hill, 1961). Pete Maslowski's "National Policy toward the Use of Black Troops in the Revolution," *South Carolina Historical Magazine*, LXXIII (1972), and Don Higginbotham's *The War of American Independence: Military Attitudes, Policies, and Practice, 1763-1789* (New York, 1971) provide background information on the employment of black troops in the Continental Army. Black loyalists have received a fair reappraisal from James W. St. G. Walker, "Blacks as American Loyalists: The Slaves' War for Independence," *Historical Reflections*, II (1975), and

Mary Beth Norton, "The Fate of Some Black Loyalists of the American Revolution," *Journal of Negro History*, LVIII (1973). The Cornwallis Papers at the Library of Congress; Revolutionary Pension Claims at the National Archives; Secretary of State, Revolutionary Military Papers at the North Carolina State Archives; and the American Loyalist Claims in the collections of both the English Records and British Records at the State Archives all yield materials on the black experience in the Revolution. The following works are also helpful: Albert R. Newsome (ed.), "A British Orderly Book, 1780-1781," *North Carolina Historical Review*, IX (1932); Leora H. McEachern and Isabel M. Williams (eds.), *Wilmington-New Hanover Safety Committee Minutes, 1774-1776* (Wilmington, 1974); and *Report of American Manuscripts in the Royal Institutions of Great Britain* (London and Dublin, 4 vols., 1904-1909).

ABOUT THE AUTHOR

Jeffrey J. Crow, a native of Akron, Ohio, received his Ph.D. in 1974 from Duke University, where he was elected to Phi Beta Kappa. Among his other publications are *Maverick Republican in the Old North State: A Political Biography of Daniel L. Russell* (Baton Rouge: Louisiana State University Press, 1977), coauthored with Robert F. Durden, and *The Southern Experience in the American Revolution* (Chapel Hill: University of North Carolina Press, 1978), coauthored with Larry E. Tise. Dr. Crow's article "Slave Rebelliousness and Social Conflict in North Carolina, 1775 to 1802," which grew out of research for this booklet, received the Daughters of Colonial Wars Award for the best article published in the *William and Mary Quarterly* in 1980. Currently Dr. Crow is director of the North Carolina Division of Archives and History.